How I Escaped

A Guide to Avoid the Pitfalls of Urban America

By

Manson M. Williams

Acknowledgement

This book was birthed through a personal quest to find true purpose in my life. During this quest, I realized that ultimately I enjoy helping people and seeing them succeed in life. I've come to understand that one of the purposes of my life is to share my life experiences to assist someone else in avoiding pitfalls.

First and foremost, thank you to my beautiful wife Karren, you have shown me a different side of life. You have provided stability and support throughout all our years together, your feedback during this writing process was invaluable.

To my kids, Nasya, Noah, and Nyomi, you are the reason I strive for greatness. Thanks for being wonderful and asking about daddy's book consistently. What you didn't know is your inquiries helped me push through to get it done.

To my parents: Dad, may you rest easy in heaven, instilling greatness in me early has paid off tremendously. Thanks for communicating the pitfalls of our environment and providing tools to assist with navigating this world. Dad, we struggled but I know you loved me. Mom, thanks for being the most faithful and loyal individual I have encountered in this world. Mom, you are a constant example of consistency and hard work.

To all my family who had great influence in my life, I thank you because in so many cases you were willing to keep me out of trouble. Even when you were in worse situations, you used it as a teaching moment to keep me from the same path.

To my friends and extended family, you have been nothing short of a GODsend. Your positive influence and support throughout my life has been much appreciated. In those times where life looked bleak, you picked me up with love and support.

Introduction

I've always wondered how fast my goals could have been achieved, had roadblocks and pitfalls been removed in my life. I grew up poor in the inner city of Detroit, Michigan during a drug epidemic that left many families in disarray, even my own. I realize as an adult that growing up in poverty without a clear guide or representation of success outside of criminal activity is damning to any community. This type of environment breeds a mindset that is unproductive within a community but also excludes you from the world outside of it. As a child, I didn't know there was better in the world; all I could see was the situation in front of me. What I was faced with on a daily basis was sad and depressing and it almost killed me.

Like an organism, I looked for ways to survive in my environment but instead of devouring my fellow inhabitants, I was set on a greater course, one geared towards learning from others mistake, education, and love. During my life journey, I realized everyone needs an opportunity to grow and live their best life. Gaining the knowledge and experience of others without incurring some of the damage that goes along with it is priceless. Everyone is presented with life altering decisions that can change their lives forever. Life happens but if you are prepared with the proper information and guidance, it makes the journey a little less painful. The bad decisions and situations of others must be your roadmap out. The road will have roadblocks and potholes, looking to slow you down, creating detours. It will happen, that's life but you must stay on the road to success.

If a person walks around the corner into a dark alley and gets robbed, would you go down the same alley? Obviously the risk of getting robbed in the same dark alley is higher than taking a heavily lit path to your destination. It's the same with life so many people have walked the same dark path before you. Instead of making uninformed decisions, you are able to reduce the amount of time it takes to accomplish goals because of someone else's knowledge and experiences. Why not learn from other peoples mistakes so your life can be a bit smoother? It's nothing wrong with benefiting from someone else's pitfall. The majority of people, who have gone through tough situations, would want you to avoid those pitfalls. This is to everyone's advantage, if you can learn from others, you must. Urban America is plagued with an unhealthy vision because of poverty, illiteracy, and lack of positive guidance just to name a few. The Urban environment is lowering people's productivity, stifling and eliminating its residents before a dream is formulated or realized. The systemic destruction of people and communities must stop and instead of change coming from external entities, it must start internally.

People like me who escaped a bad neighborhood or a dire situation had support and guidance; others had to figure it out, both made the choice to survive and do better. The reason I wrote this book is to help others escape.

Table of Contents

Escape Through Faith in GOD

The ability to develop a strong faith and personal relationship with GOD is not only critical to your success but to your overall well-being. When people fail to provide what you need in those critical moments in life, a relationship with GOD will help you get to the next level. Sometimes getting to the next step is all that's required to measure some success. Faith in a higher power allows you to call on an entity that is greater than any person or situation on this planet. The option to speak directly to the real CEO is powerful, so use that telephone line early and often.

Embrace the process of becoming a better person. The process is not always pleasant and can seem to last a lifetime, but it's a lifelong pursuit. All of your insecurities, doubt, pain, and other uncomfortable feelings that keep you from realizing your greatness will be magnified in these times, but they will eventually pass. All of the hard times I've ever experienced in life eventually were better with time. I always kept faith in GOD to lift me up. I decided to have faith that my life could be better. However, faith and believing in a higher power will not be enough to get you out of your situation, there must be action. Too many times I've seen people waiting for a higher power to bless them without any action. If you do not get off your butt and work toward your goals, you will not likely escape your situation. Faith alone is not enough.

GOD has given you talents that need to be used and targeted toward your greatness—whatever that may be.

The purpose and the answer is usually within yourself, but when you merge those positive internal messages that are within while surrounding yourself with positive people, your gift will find a way out. When unforeseen events and scenarios present themselves in life, you must have faith that things can and will get better for you. Deal with the issue in front of you and remain subjective about what needs to be done to overcome this roadblock. Do not be afraid to discuss your pitfalls or feelings with someone you trust in order to rise above it.

Some people are religious and that's great because they are usually living to a standard that allows them to do good in the world. However, there are some people in the world who are religious that manipulate their discipline to commit evil. From my perspective, religion never stopped all the bad and negative things that happened to me and my family. Religion never helped my dad kick his addiction and all the things that came along with it. All of the people who were committing foul acts in my eyes adopted religion but didn't live by principles outlined in their respective books (whether it was a Quran or the Bible).

Whatever religion you choose in your life, decipher all the good from it. Never use it for negativity. Whatever your religion, it should assist you with your spirituality and faith to promote a higher power that is looking out for you every step of the way. All my experiences, good and bad, made me more spiritual and faithful. For instance, if I didn't believe a higher power was looking out for me, how could I explain the time someone tried to shoot me? I was able to walk away from that shooting without a scratch. That traumatic situation helped me to connect with a higher power, to appreciate where I was placed in this world, and gain the strength and conviction to get me out of it.

In times of doubt, being able to pray and ask for help or forgiveness will assist in helping you escape internal and external influences that will try to keep you down. There will be plenty of times in life where you will want to quit. There will be constant barriers and roadblocks because it's not easy to pull yourself out of the mud with several people sitting on your back. But, knowing you are not alone and that GOD has your back, will serve as a very powerful tool for you spiritually, mentally, physically, and emotionally. Place your faith in a higher power because all humans are flawed. Sometimes we place expectations on people who are not worthy, but GOD is always worthy.

Escape Through Attitude

If you are looking to avoid the pitfalls of Urban America and become successful, you must learn how to maintain a positive attitude through adversity. The moment you wake up in the morning, say to yourself, "I am going to make the best out of this day in a positive way."

Attitude is a critical attribute for any individual, especially those growing up in the inner city. The attitude of a young man or woman can determine the course of his or her life very early on. Unfortunately, a positive attitude can be one of the hardest attributes to maintain when living in the inner city: The economy is not the best; your situation is often dire, and a feeling of hopelessness can continue to settle into your psyche. These scenarios will beat you down until your outlook is locked into a negative state. Once you succumb to this negative state, you are susceptible to the many ills that can befall individuals who are living in Urban America.

I want you to fight the urge of being a negative individual. I know the world feels hopeless but you have purpose in this world. Foreigners come to America with only the clothes they have on their backs and a dream. They come to America and make something of themselves because they have a positive outlook on life. Some of these individuals leave their families behind, not seeing their loved ones for years while they try to make a life for themselves in America. Most of these individuals migrate to this country from worse circumstances than anyone in America could imagine. I've met people who have come over to America unable to speak English, but they are striving to live the dream because they have chosen to approach life with a positive attitude.

I am not downplaying the inner city because I was raised in poverty on the east side of Detroit. A sense of hopelessness was part of my everyday life. But, if an individual can come from another country without speaking the English language and with very little resources to make something of themselves, then so can you! People from other countries may have to board two boats and three planes to get here, yet you were born in the land of opportunity and can't thrive because most of the time your outlook on life isn't positive.

People with negative attitudes attract others that have fallen into the same state, which creates an atmosphere of bad intentions for themselves and others. Negativity breeds negativity, and there are plenty of people who are willing to meet that negative energy with opposition. For example, if you are walking around with a negative attitude toward people, and one day you're hanging with friends and you look at the wrong person with an unwelcoming stare or what some call "mean mugging," you can put yourself into a dangerous situation. Let's say the person that you mean mug has the same negative energy, but is carrying a gun. This quickly escalates the situation. Words are exchanged, and they pull out a gun to shoot you. Based on this example, do you see how an avoidable situation can turn into a tragic one simply by possessing the wrong attitude?

Unfortunately, the example I've just presented is a sad truth for many families that are mourning loss. There are so many people who have ended up dead or in jail by having the wrong approach and attitude in their daily lives. Sometimes, we make a conscious decision to possess a negative attitude because we feel that's the only way we can survive our circumstances and our environment. It's hard to see the brighter side of things when you are growing up in circumstances that do not promote positivity. In these situations, you have to fight for positivity, especially growing up in the inner city.

In my life, I was challenged to have a positive outlook. I held onto a negative attitude as a young man, and my poor attitude really started to take hold of me in middle school. All of my exposure to criminal activity and having to grow up fast took a toll on my personality. During this time in my life, not caring helped me get through my difficult times.

I was living out a nightmare at home. Drugs were rampant in my neighborhood. Along with narcotics came violence and murder. Blaring sirens throughout my Detroit neighborhood was a constant. It was a war zone in the 1980s and 1990s. I often felt life was hopeless. My attitude started reflecting the negativity that was my surroundings.

My family had gone through the trauma of having several family members murdered within a short period of time from one another. Experiencing the loss of young uncles and aunts made me feel like life would be short. When I felt life was going to be short, I tended not to care as much. This only added fuel to the fire and enhanced my negative disposition and attitude.

My father, who was my hero, turned to drugs and after losing his siblings, he became even worse. My dad was a very complex man. He would give you the shirt off his back but he could also be the most self-centered person you've ever come across. Once the drugs took over, he was a shell of his former self, and although he continued to show love to his kids, he was failing in various aspects of raising balanced children. The leader must lead by example, but because of his habit, critical fatherly lessons slipped through the cracks.

If you know anyone that has battled with substance abuse for any period of time, then you know this individual's outlook on life, even if positivity is desired, will more than likely be bogged down by negativity. The abuser realizes their failures and decisions are affecting people, who love and depend on them, but possess no clear path to stopping the negative behavior. So, instead of my dad being accountable for his actions, he would often blame the economy, the government, or any other scapegoat to avoid looking in the mirror. This lack of accountability created a weird dynamic in my household. When I found out my dad had a problem I was shocked, sad, and confused but I still continued to listen and respect him. As years went by, those initial emotions turned to anger.

I experienced plenty of material loss due to his drug habit. This made me angry and I developed a strong distain for my dad and life. There was no running away from the problem. I had to deal with the ups and downs. I trained my mind to imagine and dream in order to escape my reality. Realistically, as a child, I couldn't limit exposure to circumstances surrounding my parents; you will face the same dilemma. Parents are precious and should be cherished. You only get one set of parents if you are lucky, but let's face it; there are plenty of people that GOD allows to have kids who fall short of their parental duties.

Some folks should have to fill out an application and go through a screening process in order to have kids. We see it every day on the news and social media: Parents prompting their kids to do everything under the sun—including murder. If this is your current situation, it's pretty extreme. But, know this, if your parent is prompting you to do something that is against the law—like shooting up a house or murder—it is obvious you need to seek help immediately. In these cases where it doesn't feel right, and there is an ability to limit a negative parent from emotional access into your life, *do* it.

I use parents in this example because I want to really drive home a point: Say no to negative people in your life, no matter who they are. In this chapter, I want the parents to realize the damage that is done to a child when unhealthy energy is projected into their lives. This is important, parents: I want to express that you are the most influential person in your child's life, so when you instill positivity in them, it will last a lifetime.

I promise these positive attributes will carry them through life. The positive thinking and outlook on life will allow them to persevere through the hard times we all know will occur. Life is short and should not be filled with negativity and misery. Every day that you wake up is another day that GOD granted you to be successful. Even if you've hit a rough patch in life, you can choose to have joy in your heart. I am telling you today that if you truly make a decision to have positivity and joy in your heart, you will be a success. That positivity will radiate and create wonders in your life. The joy in your heart will not only make you successful but it will spread to others.

There are unexplainable events in the world, but most incidents can be avoided if people decide to have a positive attitude and perspective. Don't get down on yourself because something didn't go right for you. Always look for the lesson in every situation. As you grow from an adolescent to adulthood, you should evolve. There are different variations of attitudes witnessed in life, and I want to highlight a few that I've encountered so far. I've also taken the liberty to provide insight on positive ways to view these attitudes that may have developed over your years on this earth.

Some of us have been living our entire lives with these bad attitudes, while others exhibit them in certain situations. The key is acknowledging the behavior and poor outlook, deploying what I call "attitude countermeasures" in place. If you search for the

definition of the word "countermeasure," it is simply an act taken to counteract a danger or threat. Well, ladies and gentlemen, a negative attitude is definitely a threat to all that is good in this world—everything you deserve.

Take, for example, the fields of engineering and manufacturing. Project management is prevalent in these fields of work, so problems can be easily identified which may become a roadblock from meeting a schedule, a cost, or both. Countermeasures are put in place to get the project back on track. I have taken these methodologies and tools and applied them to my everyday life so that when my attitude is not the best, or I am faced with a situation that is the root cause of my negative attitude, I have a countermeasure ready. I implement a countermeasure to get my mind back on track and focused on positivity, on the things that really matter. Unhealthy thoughts will run through your mind, and these thoughts will magnify your insecurities, keeping you weak and vulnerable. You must condition yourself to take action immediately, silencing these thoughts quickly. If you allow an unhealthy thought process to settle into your psyche, it will drag you down deep into a hole from which you may never emerge.

Life in the inner city can be a harsh reality for some. It feels like a dark cloud hovering over the city, and you start to develop the perception that something or someone is holding you back. The letdowns in life are plentiful in these communities, and it begins at a young age. Think about all the things you see advertised on television for sale: our parents can't afford to buy these things for you, and promises are made that aren't kept on birthdays and Christmas. Once a kid is let down numerous times, purposely or inadvertently, the child will start to develop coping mechanisms.

These mechanisms can drive deficiencies within a child, and it can start with something as seemingly insignificant as lying to their friends at school about what presents they got because they don't want to feel left out or less than to their classmates. This is where the "I-don't-care" attitude starts to develop. This "I-don't-care" attitude type keeps a person from dealing with the realities of life because every time something bad happens, instead of dealing with the issue, you simply state, "I don't care." This statement is very powerful because it starts off as a defense mechanism, but then it begins to take over your thought processes and feelings toward life. It starts with a light-hearted "I don't care" then morphs into the "I-don't-care-if-I-die-or-go-to-jail" scenario.

Stay away from the "I-don't-care" attitude. Parents, teach your kids early to care about themselves and help them to understand that material things *do not* make them. Teach, coach, and mentor your children to care about their education, their lives, and their freedom. The "I don't care" is contagious. It spreads like a nasty disease amongst people. It's easier to say I don't care, but that's the coward's way. It will destroy children and adults the same each day. It will shred the fabric of any valuable relationship because this attitude will not allow for the compassion that's required to maintain high-quality relationships. These high-quality relationships are needed to avoid the pitfalls. Get rid of the "I don't care" and change it to an "I-do-care" attitude. I do care about my education. I do care about my future. I do care about being a productive member of society.

My attitude was pretty bad as a youngster. The "I-don't-care" mentality had set in for me and for many of the people around me. I was a victim of circumstances and environment. I felt life tearing me down as a middle schooler. I was in a situation where those above me should have been pulling me up, but life was pulling me in a negative direction. I often struggled with a feeling of hopelessness.

My father tried his best to motivate me, but his methods were not always practical. Of course, every human being deals with unfortunate life circumstances, but sometimes these burdens seem unfairly distributed to those who are unprepared or untrained for life's obstacles.

When the decision is made to lead a life that is full, it will not always be easy because so many people in today's society gravitate toward negativity. The gravitation toward negativity is evident everywhere in our daily lives—from family members and to co-workers, to social media feeds and news outlets. The negative stories get all the press while positivity gets little to no air play.

Choosing to look at the brighter side of things and to have a positive attitude requires discipline and restraint. Choosing to react negatively toward an individual or situation is too easy, and choosing to take the high road in tense situations will challenge you. But you should constantly challenge yourself to be a better person. I challenge myself to speak to everyone in passing. I don't care if it's the janitor or a CEO, they both put their pants on one leg at a time, and they both deserve my respect.

Sometimes you will come into contact with people that have poor dispositions and they try to bring you into their realm of sorrow and misery, but don't take the bait. Challenge yourself to be positive in that person's presence and your attitude and energy will allow you to shine. Regardless of what anyone says or thinks, people like to deal with someone with a positive attitude. A positive attitude will pull you through a lot of situations. It can be the difference between getting that promotion you are seeking or not. It can be a deciding factor in whether you get the "hook up" in your favorite establishment. I've learned in life, if you are kind to people; they will typically reciprocate the favor.

Get rid of the "everybody-is-against-me" attitude. Always remember, you can't control who likes you. There are plenty of reasons in the world someone may decide not to like you, that's their problem, not yours. Sometimes it's just your insecurities that allow you to believe someone doesn't like you or that an individual is acting a certain way. I've encountered people and situations where my initial assessment of them was wrong. Never limit yourself, be open to meet all people from all walks of life. If not, this could be a hindrance to your growth. In some cases, there are people that are against you, use a conflict resolution method for these situations. Most times, avoidance can work if this person has no direct involvement in your life. If you are worried about who likes you in life, you will never be successful. You could be the most likeable person on Earth, but there will still be someone who doesn't like you for whatever reason. So, don't worry about who likes you because it's a puzzle you will never be able to solve. Stop being the person that believes everybody has something against you, in exchange for refusing to take accountability for your own actions. If you are a student getting bad grades in school and wonder why, stop making up excuses! Since the beginning of structured classrooms—or at least as far back as when I was a kid—parents have heard children complain, "My teacher doesn't care for me." I' personally used this line with my parents as a youngster. If you were paying attention and not talking during instruction maybe your teacher *would* like you. I bet the teacher would actually adore you.

Believe me, the people I know that are educators aren't in the profession to become rich. It's because they want to see kids have a bright future. The least their students can do is give them their full attention during instruction. The people you think like you may not like you at all. Those who you perceive to not care for you probably do, but instead of spending valuable bandwidth on trying to figure either of these out, just be the great individual you were put on this earth to be, and be *you*. Start looking at success as a way to show people that you are worthy of being "hated on" as my peers use to say back in our college days. Give the people something worthy to "hate on" you for. If you're not graduating from high school, going to college, taking up a trade, or launching a business, then no one will hate on your accomplishments. Give the world something to hate on.

You have to be accountable for your own actions and progress in life. This applies to people of all ages because sometimes we fall back into a space where we are blaming other people for our bad decisions. Life presents a countless number of roadblocks that are not always avoidable. In life, you will lose loved ones unexpectedly; people are going to disappoint you—even the people that are supposed to protect you. Being equipped with the understanding that life will happen and developing a mindset preparing for such events will assist you during these difficult times.

You should pray often, and love the people most precious to you every day because tomorrow isn't promised. I learned this lesson the hard way when I was 11 years old. When I was leaving my grandfather's downstairs flat, my uncle was letting us out the door so we could go to my cousin's basketball game. It was a wintery day, with light snow on the ground. I did something I'd never done before, as I was the last person out the door: I turned to my uncle and gave him a hug and told him that I loved him. He was a rough and tough guy who had been through everything imaginable from going to prison for 10-plus years to recovering from being shot multiple times. He embraced me and said, he loved me too. That was the last time that I would see my uncle Butchie alive. He was murdered later that same afternoon.

My uncle's death was one of the saddest experiences of my life because it was my first experience of physically touching someone without any thought of not seeing them again on Earth. One minute my uncle was giving me a hug, and the next he was no longer here with me. I was totally unprepared for a situation like this, and unfortunately it wasn't the last experience like this in my life.

An individual will never get used to losing people, especially violently, but the mind and heart must protect itself. These situations in life will drive you into a negative direction, but you must use these life lessons to shape your destiny. Initially, bad experiences in my life shaped my attitude in a negative way, but one thing I learned from my uncle's murder was to avoid situations and people who could bring misery to my doorstep.

I didn't want to put myself in positions where I heightened the risk of shortening my life or anyone in my family's life. Besides, I didn't have to. I had enough crazy family members who would take up the slack. In these instances in life, it can become difficult not to adopt the "everybody-is-against-me" attitude because in dire times and situations, the feeling is so real. But, everybody is not against you, and most times it's the situations that we put ourselves in that lead us to feel this way.

Unfortunately, my uncle wasn't innocent. Although no one deserves to get murdered, his attitude and outlook on life directly affected the outcome. Life happens and things don't work out the way you plan. It doesn't mean everybody is against you.

For instance, just because your parents won't allow you to do what you want doesn't mean they don't have your best interest in mind. Remember, all parents have gone through exactly what you are going through. So, if they feel that something you want to do can be detrimental to your future, then it's probably in your best interest to take heed. America needs to know that circumstances can be changed when you commit to being somebody, living with purpose, and having the right attitude. Let the star shine instead of impeding its brightness. Give yourself the opportunity to shine. Everybody is not against you. If you believe in yourself and GOD is for you, how can you lose?

It's true, kids are misused and abused. I've experienced and witnessed it too many times. I've known parents who were not worthy and did not show their kids love. My parents weren't always the loving individuals I deserved and required, but they showed just enough love where the disappointment caused by them would not completely derail my life. Besides, as a young boy I developed a way to look at things from a positive perspective. Although I was beat down mentally and physically at times, the dream of becoming something greater than what my environment dictated was stronger than anything.

Love is an action word, you cannot tell a person you love them and not show it. "Nobody ever loved me" can be very real for some people; kids get discarded in the system all the time. The root cause of this attitude is parents not loving their kids as they should. Kids start acting out and seeking love in the wrong places which makes them more susceptible to being in bad situations.

Parents face the possibility of their child being targeted by human traffickers, especially those with daughters. With new technology and social media, it makes accessing a child easier for these predators. If a child lacks a positive outlook on life, feels unloved, or lives without confidence, the risk is greater for that child to fall into the hands of one of these predators. The trafficker is looking for these characteristics so they can target a child and once they lure them to a place, they will be under the control of these individuals. They will never be the same—possibly never to be seen again— and scarred for life during this experience.

So, parents, develop a positive attitude about how you raise your children. Your attitude should be geared toward loving that child and making sure they are not abused by you and certainly not any predators looking to destroy the gift that GOD gave you. Their upbringing should be something you cherish. A child should never feel like no one ever loved them. This attitude breed's disdain with the rest of the world because they may feel everyone else is receiving love except for them. It starts off with sadness and can turn to hate. Self-esteem issues can be devastating to an individual, and if the foundation is weak, then it makes for a weaker adult.

Parents who were not shown love should take extra steps to care for their children because, ultimately, they understand what it feels like not to have that love. In the urban community, there are so many parents that do not step up to the plate. Absent fathers are rampant, but there are neglectful mothers too. Just because you're there doesn't mean you're nurturing a child correctly. Do not fall into this type of mindset and attitude, remember if no one else loves you, GOD does, take that love and be all that GOD intended you to be.

Some of you may read this and think, *What does GOD have to do with these situations*? GOD has everything to do with your life. You need GOD to govern your actions for what's good and bad in life. Human beings will let you down because it's part of the experience of being flawed. Nobody is perfect, but if you put your faith in GOD, then you won't be let down. The natural ability for you to succeed is within you. It's GOD given, but you have to tap into the resource within you and strive for greatness. For those that don't believe because they can't see GOD, I say to you, "You can't see air but you need it to breathe."

Escape Through Education

The "school-isn't-for-me" attitude is a dangerous disposition to have in today's society. Currently, we live in a society where blue-collar jobs are not plentiful like they were back when America experienced a big industrial boom in the 1900s. The average American nowadays cannot live a middle-class lifestyle without some type of education. When manufacturing was booming in America, people of all backgrounds could go out and find high-paying factory jobs. If they were dissatisfied with that company, they could go to the next factory down the street. These jobs were available for high school graduates and people could afford to take a, "school is not for me" attitude. Most people could make the same if not more money than an individual that went away and spent thousands of dollars on a college degree.

The world is forever changing so you have to evolve with it. Education is now the cornerstone to a better life in America. During America's transformation into the Information Age, education is a requirement. There are a number of millionaires and billionaires who dropped out of college and pursued business, but these individuals make up a small percentage of the world. Outliers like Bill Gates, possessing the genius and vision to create and innovate at the right moment in time comes once in a life time, however it's not impossible for you to create something just as innovative if you work hard. I wanted to be like Michael Jordan when I was younger just like millions of other kids around the world, but I wasn't going to be 6 foot 6 or possess his athletic ability. It was more likely that I could become an Engineer. If you possess athletic ability, by all means pursue it with all you have but always educate yourself, you will need it whether you succeed in sports or not. If you want a better life, make EDUCATION FOR YOU!

Poverty is real in the U.S., especially for individuals working a minimum-wage job. One reason why adults find themselves working minimum-wage jobs most times is because education wasn't a priority. A four year degree is not always the answer but any field garnering a descent salary will require some form of education. You will be doomed to a life of barely getting by, even when working 40-plus hours a week, unless you get a good paying factory job, if you don't have some type of education. Unfortunately, those jobs are usually limited and require some type of referral to apply and receive a call-back. The lower paying jobs will still keep you under the poverty guidelines because taxes must come out of your check. Health benefits are also another expense. By the time, all the deductions are subtracted there isn't much income left to live on. I don't think anybody in their right mind wants to live in poverty.

The problem is, Urban America is not educated on all the ways to make life profitable which keeps people from living a better life. Life is not enjoyable when you work like a dog and the lights are still being cut off, you can barely pay the landlord, or keep the gas on in the house. Know this, the "school-isn't-for-me" attitude will have an adverse effect on your life. No education means, no experiences outside of working to pay the bills. You may know it as the "rat race," a vicious cycle in America where you work to pay bills, living from paycheck to paycheck. The "rat race" applies to many Americans who are educated as well, of course, but those who are uneducated are more susceptible. The only difference is those with an education are probably living a little better, making a nice salary but with higher expenses.

I know you don't want to live like this, so make education a priority for you. Being educated helps break the cycle within your family if everyone before you took the "school-is-not-for-me" road. I want you to stop reading this book for just a second and shout as loud as you can: *School is for me!* Make a habit of training yourself to understand that education is the key to freedom and a better life.

If there are any programs in your area where you can spend most of your time reading, studying, exercising, it is imperative that you seek them out. In my case, throughout the chaos, my mom would make sure I was signed up for programs like the Detroit Area Pre-College Engineering Program (DAPCEP) which was held at Wayne State University located in the midtown area of Detroit. DAPCEP exposed me to a college campus which gave me a different outlook on life. Besides traveling to the west side to see my grandmother, I was not familiar with any other parts of town except for the couple of blocks I was allowed to visit on the east side near my home.

Having an opportunity to catch the bus to a college campus located fifteen minutes from where I lived was a big adventure for me as an eighth-grade student. It was unbelievable how life could be so different if you traveled only a few miles east, west, north, or south. It was a totally different world—a far cry from the "dope boys" standing on my corner selling drugs. On campus there were no sounds of gun fire or screeching cars leaving the scenes of drive-by shootings. Once I got off the cross -town bus on Forest, there were college students shuffling back and forth, looking to make an impact on the world and I knew that's what I wanted to do. I didn't want to be a part of making the world a worse place to live.

The experience opened my eyes to the possibility of attending a University and it also exposed me to different students who came from families without a history of criminal activity and those influences assisted with my dream of making something of myself and getting out of the hood. The DAPCEP experience helped me believe that my dream of becoming an engineer was actually achievable. We mainly focused on math and science throughout the six-to-eight-week program with a project to complete before the program concluded. The program made me a stronger student, and it gave me an outlet to escape the chaos of my neighborhood. If there isn't a parent to assist you, request information from a student counselor at school. But, you must grow up and commit to yourself. Commit to experiencing a life outside of what you know from being oppressed in a ghetto. Don't be afraid to be educated and to want more for your life. If I didn't graduate from high school and go on to obtain a four-year degree in Manufacturing Engineering and later a Master's in business, my life would have been totally different.

Initially, I started my high school career at my neighborhood school. Kids were getting high, gambling, and drinking. There was an abundance of negativity inside of this school. A place where I needed to learn was a cesspool for illegal activity. Instead of being eager to learn, I was worried about whether or not I would get beat up by a group of guys, robbed, or shot. Luckily, I was able to get out of that situation. Thanks to my parents who never gave up on getting me into a decent school! Parents, please get your child into the best school possible. It really makes a big difference in their lives. Although it may inconvenience the family, it's worth the sacrifice. By going to a school outside of my neighborhood, it helped me meet people from different walks of life all around the city. Many of these people came from decent backgrounds and were a positive influence on me. The schools with higher expectations enroll students who have similar goals. Students were looking to avoid the cycle of drugs and violence through education. There are always going to be some bad apples, but not nearly as many when you attend a school with high standards and expectations.

Plead with your parents to get you out of that difficult situation, and if there are no other options, you need to find the positive people in your school and make an alliance. Those positive kids will make an unimaginable impact in your life. Not only will these friends impact your life, but they may have parents or older siblings whose influence is irrefutable—the possibilities for great connections are endless.

I really started to understand what education was doing for me during high school. I was able to meet people who were on a good path.

My core group of friends in high school became my confidants, and eventually my "brothers and sisters". Although I never revealed a lot about what was going on in my life going to a High school where I felt relatively safe with good people made a world of difference in my life. It was a break from all the madness at my house and neighborhood.

There was no blueprint for me. "Go to school and get an education" was the advice I received from my parents. Some of you don't have any guidance. You may be the first person to learn on a higher level in your family. That's all right, just be sure to step up to the challenge! Sometimes, the only individuals who can understand your struggles are people strategically put in place so that you can help one another grow.

When I was in high-school, I would overhear some of my peers say that college wasn't for them so they didn't attend. Even when I arrived at college I heard some say the same thing. They were there only half-heartedly, putting forth no effort to go to class or make the most of their opportunity. An education is priceless and in today's society, it's very difficult to lead a great quality of life without some type of continual education after high school.

GOD blessed me with the right friends during the times where I needed them most. We often put our heads together to solve problems. If we needed clothes for homecoming, we scraped up money, hustled, and borrowed from one another to make it happen. One homecoming my friend placed a whole outfit on a credit card for me during our senior year because I didn't have the money. I had to pay him back of course. Lord knows what he was doing with a credit card, but the fact remains that because of my friend; I didn't have to risk my life or freedom trying to get an outfit for homecoming. I know what you're thinking, "Risk your life for an outfit?" But, it was that serious and people lost their lives for much less in our neighborhoods.

All my friends had dreams of going off to college because that was the natural progression for us. Either attend college, or take up a trade by working for one of the automakers or an automotive supplier. The other option—but no option for us—was to become a drug dealer, because that was Detroit's second biggest industry after automotive. It would have been immoral

32

from any standpoint for me to pick up a bag of crack. I personally witnessed all the destruction firsthand with a parent and family members battling drug addictions. While the influences to gravitate towards drugs were very strong, I continued surrounding myself with the right people and became a leader. It paid off for me as I grew and I started to find my identity.

Our friendships in high school weren't perfect, nor were any of us—we were just trying to survive, and navigate through unchartered territory without a compass. But, we *were* trying. It made a huge difference. Not settling, but trying—striving—for something better, something more. Once I grasped an understanding of how pertinent positive people are, it became a focal point for me.

Martin Luther King Jr. High school had some awesome teachers and counselors who were willing to go above and beyond for their students. I've always been grateful for them because where our parents lacked they picked up some of the slack. I remember my best friend and I were completing college applications, and the entire process to attend college was unchartered territory for us. My parents never went to college and I had minimal contact with family members on my mother's side who completed college. I decided to apply at Western Michigan University, Central Michigan University, and Prairie View in Texas. I was accepted to all of the universities where I applied, but I chose Western because my best friend was accepted as well and it made sense for us to take the journey together.

We both wanted to go into Engineering—mainly because we wanted to make a lot of money! Our situation was so crazy, that neither one of us had a way to make it to orientation to start at Western. My parents couldn't take us because they didn't have a car in the household. We could never keep a car. When we had a vehicle, my dad would run it into the ground. GOD places people in your life that can assist with certain things—to help finish your race—and, in this case, that was Mrs. Lopez. Our English teacher didn't have to step up and drive us to Western, drive back home, and then come back two days later once orientation was over. But, she did and I am forever grateful.

People will seek to assist you in life, but only if they see that you are putting forth effort to help yourself. Ms. Lopez saw two young men trying to make something of themselves, it was a situation where we were limited and she decided to step in. There is strength in numbers and energy can be magnified if you focus on one common goal together.

I always say, "You don't want to grow up in any other institution other than a University." That quote is designed to express the contrast between growing up in a correctional institution or one for higher learning. The option is not always so evident for youngsters. A University is where you can grow without too many external influences. It isn't generally based on who has the most money, or whose designer clothes are best because the vast majority are broke college students just like yourself. There will always be someone with more access, but in college the playing field is more leveled, and societal pressures can be reduced because the goal for everyone is to graduate.

Once you're surrounded by like-minded people, some who have shared similar life experiences, growth happens. Being exposed to people from different cities and even countries allows you to see the world through a new set of lenses. The blocks that you stood on within an inner city will seem to expand right before your eyes. All of your excuses will suddenly become irrelevant if you have a conscious mind and truly want better for yourself. People from different ethnic backgrounds and cultures start to influence the way you view the world. The moment I arrived on campus at Western Michigan University and saw the smooth roads that seemed to be freshly paved—no litter anywhere, no liquor stores on every corner—a calm-but-exciting feeling passed through my body. There weren't any signs of imminent danger present, and at that moment I knew this would be the institution where I would grow up. Immediately, I met people who would have a lasting impact on my life. There weren't many minorities, so I coveted the ones I came across. Along with my best friend, we started our journey. We met other like-minded individuals who came from decent backgrounds, who possessed different perspectives on life—many that calmed me and taught me how to cope with life's disappointments.

If I had approached life with the attitude that *"school wasn't for me"*, I would have missed opportunities to meet and fellowship with so many wonderful people who had positive input and influence which helped to change the trajectory of my life. Even if college is not suitable for your ambitions and desires, there are alternatives. There are technical schools available that promote skilled trades which can provide you with a good life. Whatever your desire and passion, there is some legitimate way to achieve your goals and dreams without exposing yourself to violent or volatile situations.

Education and information have been simplified through the Internet, so much so that there is nothing you can't figure out in a matter of seconds. The Internet is a powerful tool that can assist you with breaking down barriers and overcoming some shortcomings in your life. For example, if you don't have transportation to take classes on campus, many universities offer classes online. There is no reason why you can't educate and elevate yourself. Get Educated!

Escape Through Accountability

People often use others as their crutch in life. Many people think to themselves, *Why didn't my parents or countless others do everything in their power to make a better life for me?* Or, *Why can't they help me to be successful?* Once you reach a certain age, you have to be accountable for yourself. Identifying other people's shortcomings when it comes to your progress will lead you down a road of self-pity and stagnation. Your parents or elders may have their own challenges, circumstances, or life experiences that may prevent them from identifying your needs.

I have seen adults who've never had love and guidance in their lives, fail to stop the cycle with their children. They fail because of their inability to not repeat the same behavior which continues the cycle. I've encountered people who made a conscious effort not to fall down the same path of destruction; in turn they have become great parents despite their upbringing. The cycle of despair tends to haunt Urban America. Be a game changer and break the cycle. Just because someone was not fair and just to you doesn't mean that behavior should be transferred to the next generation.

Generations change tremendously with the world, because the world is always evolving. My parents didn't have social media, so they were always reserved and private about their affairs. Besides that's just how you were raised: Always keep family business confidential. The younger generations have taken to social media and will publicize content that used to be considered sacred. This is an example of why you should not blame parents for any shortcomings.

Take, for example, when crack hit the streets in the early 1980s. Many baby boomers first tried it in the urban community, not knowing what it would ultimately do to them. The people in Urban America, and all around the country, believed they were just having a good time. They did not know how it would destroy their lives and ultimately affect their families and their communities for generations to come.

The "why-didn't-my-parents" attitude can stunt an individual's growth. It's expected that a child would think this way because it's the parents' duty to nurture and provide (I am not referring to these individuals). I'm talking about adults continuing to use their parents' shortcomings as an excuse not to succeed in life. I am telling you now, if your parents let you down in any way, take the challenge and uplift yourself to be better, be more.

Most parents really want the best for their kids even if they couldn't give it to them. But, I've witnessed plenty of young adults give up because that's what their parents did. Don't give up! Find that inner strength, seek out a mentor or role model, and mimic those attributes to dig yourself out of that hole of self-pity and low self-esteem. If you let go of the negative attitude and thinking, I promise you will achieve goals beyond your wildest imagination.

Escape Through Love

In order to escape through love, you must first practice self-love. Self-love will help to escape the toxicity and self-hate you may feel within and assist with identifying people and situations that are detrimental to your well-being. If self-love isn't a priority, you will be susceptible to being used and abused by people who specialize in taking advantage of others. This is how you start to break the dysfunctional cycle that continues to plague our neighborhoods. Love yourself and then become an advocate of this emotion, start with your family members. Failure to master self-love will not be fair to you or the people who will depend on you throughout a life time. If you have a deficiency in loving yourself, how can you whole heartedly love someone else? Love yourself enough to survive. Love yourself enough not to make unsound decisions that will land you in jail or get you killed. I want everyone reading this book to really focus on love for self and for others because as the saying goes, "love conquers all." Love can decrease the violence and pitfalls that a child or adult has to go through. Love for yourself is pertinent and critical to success. No one should want to go to prison or die in the street like a dog. Even if you get away with a heinous crime, no one should want to live with that horror. Loving others enough to be a better individual can be a major contributor to success. Loving my parents and not wanting to let them down helped me to stay in school (also the fact that my dad would kill me if I dropped out). I never wanted to disappoint my parents out of respect and love. I understood that it was tough raising all of us in an

impoverished and violent environment.

One of the main reasons I survived through my hardships in life was because I held onto positive thinking and people. When I was younger, I didn't have any daily role models but I had a father who poured love into me when he wasn't out in the streets. The love from my father was based on outward expressions of affection through hugs and kisses, but also his drive to see his children avoid the traps and pitfalls he experienced. My father didn't graduate from high school, but he was naturally gifted with intelligence. I could only imagine his life's potential had he chosen a different path.

Technically-speaking, my father was not a man that I would want to pattern my life after, but I respected his love for me and I took all the positive words of encouragement he had for me. My gift was the ability to listen and absorb knowledge, enhance my social IQ so that I could deal with people from all walks of life. This was particularly important if you wanted to survive in a hostile and dangerous environment.

My mother wasn't much for having a close bond with her children when I was younger, but I witnessed her go to work every day to help support our family. She showed love in different ways, and this love and compassion was intermittently displayed throughout my young life. My mother and I didn't get close until I was away at college. I remember times where my dad had to force her to give me a hug but, undoubtedly, I knew the love was there.

As a young boy, both my parents sat with me on countless days and nights, helping me with math and vocabulary flash cards, propelling me to skip kindergarten going directly to the first grade. There was a great deal of love and effort put into making me successful, and that's why I plead with any parents to make the effort to plant positive seeds and to watch their flowers blossom. Love and positivity can carry you far because there is plenty of negativity in the world designed to derail us all. Having children of my own now, I understand the fear my parents possessed in regards to my well-being growing up.

My inward love for myself eventually became so overwhelming; I no longer wanted to become successful for everyone else. I wanted to make it out of the hood for me. Revelations are discovered through various vehicles and despite the messenger; you have to love yourself enough to understand when jewels are being given to you. In those instances, I loved myself enough to take in the positivity and discard any negativity. There were days when my dad would sit on the couch high, and tell me about life. I would sit on my parents' couch and listen. He would talk about life experiences that will last a lifetime, lessons that I will hand down to my own children.

I will be the first to tell you that it's hard to love yourself in an environment where all you see is self-hate, but the alternative is self-destruction. Love is one of the critical keys to success. One of the ways to start dispelling the brutal and senseless cycle of violence in the inner city is to show love, not hate.

I challenge you to turn on the evening news, and watch each storyline in most major cities. What you will witness are senseless robberies, assaults, and murders. These crimes are obviously committed by people that do not love themselves or anyone else enough to pause and think about what heinous crime they are about to commit. So, they take a life and they go to prison for a long time, sometimes forever or sentenced to death. The news shows young inner-city kids committing these crimes every night, and then the police arrest them and judges put them in jail. Please love yourself enough to avoid being a crime statistic and become part of a more distinguished statistic: college graduate.

It may sound cliché but, as I've mentioned before, love is an action word. It's a feeling that's unmistakable when it occurs. I am sure you've heard people state that love doesn't hurt, but I beg to differ. It's unrealistic to think that love won't hurt; every human being on this earth is subject to hurting someone directly or indirectly because we are human. We are susceptible to make mistakes, and we are fallible and flawed. The trick is not to allow pain to become reoccurring in your life. If you continue to allow the same people to hurt you without learning a lesson from the pain, you will experience a difficult time.

Someone who loves you may make a mistake, but will not want to hurt you again. I want the men and, especially the women, to pay attention to the statement,

"Love does not hurt over and over again." Love doesn't steal from you. Love doesn't beat you down. Love builds you up, love keeps you safe and feeling beautiful.

The problem is there are so many children who grew up without proper role models in their lives. In the inner city, there are a lot of broken homes, usually where the father is absent. This eliminates the possibility of a child seeing their mom and dad together. The home is where a child learns how they should approach life and relationships. Kids learn by what they witness growing up. A household without a father is without two things: a model of how a man should treat a woman, and how a woman should treat a man. If both parents are present in the household and it's dysfunctional, that's a different story but can be equally destructive. The concept is the same: These children will be strongly influenced in their own relationships by what they've witnessed, and they will be faced with making a decision about whether, and how, they will break the cycle.

In the urban community, people are always saying, "I got love for you" in different variations. Maybe you've heard, "I got mad love for you" where the word "mad" is supposed to heighten the love. In your life people are going to say the words but it's their actions you need to pay close attention to because "I got mad love for you" can be accompanied with a knife in the back.

Love doesn't place you in bad situations. There are people in this world who see something in you, even when you may not see it in yourself. The inner city is a place of survival, and people will pretend to be your best friend for all sorts of reasons: just to have a companion or because they're scared and they need protection. If they can ride your coattail, they will do so until all opportunities and advantages run out.

How many young, inner city kids do you see on reality TV crime shows like, *The Next 48*? These individuals pretend to be down with the Thug Life, but when they get arrested and have to sit alone in an interrogation room all the love goes away for their so-called homie or home girl. It never fails; the person will start to tell before commercial break. Someone who loves you wouldn't put you in a position where you would have to be involved with the police. Take yourself and your loved ones out of situations where their lives can be ruined by the judicial system. Once you're in the system, it's almost impossible to get out. We've seen plentiful examples of how someone's life is altered because of fake love. These so-called friends and family are people who know how to hide and deceive very well, so if it doesn't feel right, just stay away from that person and situation.

Many have also been blinded by the idea of love, don't fall for it. Speak with older family members—it could be a church member or someone with wisdom—ask them about their friends or family who spoke the words "I love you" but whose actions proved otherwise, most would be able to articulate a time of disappointment. Loves is an action word, and if someone is showing you something different, please take heed. It only takes one wrong decision in life and it can change forever.

I've had too many moments in my life where my quest for success could have been derailed because of my environment in Detroit. I didn't view my friends and family members as bad people although, in hindsight, some of them were. The problem was most of the people around me growing up bought into the negativity of our environment, and not enough of my elders were trying to elevate above it. Naturally, some of these legal and illegal tactics influenced my life growing up.

In my neighborhood, and all across the city, people used marijuana. The first time I ever experimented with marijuana was in middle school when I was in the eighth grade. My brother and I were walking down Chalmers (a busy street on Detroit's east side) on the way to my grandpa's house on Lakewood. My brother, two years my senior, was my confidant at the time. As we were walking, traveling south on Chalmers and crossing Canfield, he pulled out a joint. I was hesitant about using any type of drug since I watched the effects of it in my neighborhood. It was hard to get away from weed because it was everywhere and there was no escaping it. Adults fired up joints in front of kids all the time. In fact, that's where most of the kids obtained weed to smoke, from their parents' stash.

This particular day, I was feeling bad about myself; I didn't care where my brother got it from. I was so low that the thought of suicide frequently crossed my mind. So, I smoked the weed. My weed experience was lack luster, already paranoid from trying it; I immediately knew that it wasn't for me. I felt funny and distant from my problems at the time but the effects soon wore off and I was faced with the same problems. Drugs will not be an escape for your problems.

There were times where I couldn't visualize a way out of my hell, the only way out, I figured was death. Since my family was somewhat religious, my dad taught us early that killing yourself was a sin. I knew that killing myself was against GOD's will, so when my parents would send me on "errands". I often hoped someone would jump out from behind a bush and end all the pain for me.

Those were the times where I yearned to be free. I didn't care about the pain my parents would feel if something happened to me. There were times I doubted they cared anyway. I was exposed to unnecessary risk for a couple of measly, loose cigarettes or a few dollars from returned bottles just because my dad was too lazy to get up and go himself. I was tired of struggling, there needed to be an end. A lot of the missions my dad sent us on were during the night. These were very scary times: People were being murdered daily, robbed, kidnapped, raped and sometimes all three offenses at once. Too many evils lurked the streets. I felt vulnerable at times, but after completing so many missions, the soldier came out of me and I learned to do what was necessary.

GOD was in my heart, and I always believed that but there were times when doubt would settle into my mind. I would ask myself, *Why would GOD allow a good kid or any child to suffer through this type of environment?* Although, I often didn't agree with my parents, I always remained respectful. Honestly, I didn't have a choice because both of them would punish me tremendously if I stepped out of line. As I grew older, there were times that warranted me really lashing out at my parents, but I always took the high road. I didn't want to judge them because on some level, they were doing the best with what they were given. It's just too bad their best was sometimes the worst.

Because I knew my parents had internal pain and disappointment that wasn't addressed in their lives, it helped me to better understand my situation. My siblings and I were direct or indirect recipients of all their pain and disappointment. This is when I realized I had to start understanding the psychology and history behind what was happening to me. I would sit and talk with my dad; he would go through several emotions in one discussion. His pain ran deep and when he hurt, we all felt the pain. I loved my dad; our talks would be so intense and emotional, but I started to resent them after a while. A good day would easily swing in the wrong direction during a discussion.

If you are a parent, be cognizant of your issues. Go talk

to a professional about your issues. Discuss the pain of an absent parent, or any form of abuse you've encountered in your life. Do whatever you can to be able to project love into your child's life. Kids, be in love with yourself. Know that you will make it, and don't worry about what someone else thinks about you. Be everything that you were intended to be. If your mom or dad is not in your life and they are alive, then you have even more of a reason to love yourself. Love yourself and use any disappointment to fuel your motivation to be great!

This world can be very scary, especially when you don't have the comfort of a nice neighborhood or money to purchase all the needed essentials. In my situation, I started to view myself as a gladiator because I had to build up a mental, physical, and emotional toughness to get through life. I also added love to the equation because as a gladiator, you need to understand the right amount of love required for any situation. Love for yourself first and foremost, then your family and friends. It's alright to be a gladiator for love as long as it doesn't hurt you. If you become a gladiator for love, it will be reciprocated throughout your life.

There are so many people I've come across in life who don't remember me because of how tough I was, but for how I showed them love, how I added to their lives— even if it was just simple words of kindness when they may have needed them most. Become a balanced gladiator. Build yourself physically, emotionally, and mentally, keep the right amount of toughness weighed against an equal amount of love.

I am reminded of the stories of LeBron James and Shaquille O'Neal whose biological fathers were absent. These kids grew up to be successful men with riches that maybe only one percent of the world can fathom. I don't know if their motivation was driven by an absent parent, but I bet those absent fathers wished they had been in their lives due to their overwhelming success. These men are just two examples who happen to be in sports and entertainment, but there are many successful professionals faced with the same circumstances. In the case of LeBron and Shaq, someone loved them, but they also had enough love for themselves to recognize their talents and whatever support system was available to push them toward their goals. I use these two athletes as examples because I followed their careers on television and read about their journeys. Shaq had a song in which he rapped the lyric, "his stepdad was his father because his biological didn't bother". When I was younger, those lyrics resonated with me and although I didn't know Shaq personally, it made me proud, he was able to achieve success despite his biological dad not being in his life. The world also knew Shaq was raised by a strong mother as well.

I've never met Lebron or Shaq but watching their careers, business, and personal profiles over the years, no one has ever stated they weren't good dads. These two stars are commendable along with any parent willing to end a poor cycle of behavior. Outside of these two examples, there are many men in the world; some that I know personally who grew up without a father in the household. These men are great dads to their own children. Love is powerful. Sometimes the lack of love increases awareness and encourages people to love stronger and deeper if they are given the opportunity.

It doesn't matter if you share genetics with someone, love sets you apart. Real love can help people heal and get through this roller coaster called life. The man who I knew as my grandfather didn't share the same blood as me. Although, some family members made it clear that he was a stepdad to my father, my grandfather always treated me fairly. My dad believed he was treated unfairly as a kid because of his status as a stepchild and there may have been some validity to his claim. My dad's beliefs shaped my thought process and I started over- analyzing things. In those instances of making a comparison in my young mind, I recognized subtle differences. Regardless, I was still grateful for the love my grandpa showed me. I still remember sitting in the living room together watching a boring Detroit Tigers baseball game. It didn't matter; I loved to spend time with him because he showed interest. The thing about love is that you need to be willing to give and receive it. There will be times in your life where you feel hardened emotionally and lack the ability to give or receive love. Do not stay in this place; find a way back to love. If you lack the strength to get back, reach out to an external entity like a place of worship because no matter what man or woman does, you have to believe that a higher power loves us all.

My grandpa was one cool dude. He was someone who was kind to me, he loved me and I could never say anything bad about him. He worked as a janitor at the hospital where I was born (Hutzel, which was close to downtown Detroit) and he would catch the bus back and forth, seeming to be a man unscathed by the violence and despair that was surrounding our neighborhood. His uniform was a green Dickies suit and it was always pressed perfectly with a crease in the pants. I remember him walking down the street with a couple bags of groceries, after stopping at Champions, the neighborhood grocery store. Champions always had a sale on chicken which was cheap back in the 80s. You could get a whole chicken for under a dollar or you could purchase a family-sized pack of hamburger. We were poor, so it was all about making the food stretch. We had a big family and a lot of us depended on grandpa to bring food home on many occasions. I always ran down the street to greet and help him carry the groceries home. Grandpa would bring home cookies for the kids and coffee—usually Folgers—for himself. We usually ate these cookies when everything else in the house was gone. We would also make coffee and put a bunch of sugar in it to enhance its taste.

He would wake up early every morning to catch the bus to work, keeping the same daily routines. I never heard him complain about it. I don't see how my grandpa maintained it all with a janitor's salary and so much demand from his family. He couldn't have anything to himself, since we ate all his cookies and even drank his coffee. I'm sure he must have been annoyed and angry at times but I never felt it was directed towards me. All I remember is the love he showed us kids, giving us a dollar or two when he received his paycheck. We would run straight to the corner store and spend it all on junk.

There are plenty of people, who would put everybody out of the house, but my grandpa was the patriarch of the family and he was doing the best he could. Although, I heard stories of my grandpa not being such a great man in his younger days, he definitely tried to make it up to his grandkids. I've learned in life to draw my own conclusions about love, and there was definitely love coming from my grandpa. He was the only person other than my uncle and my mother whom I saw go to work every day. I appreciated them because they tried their hardest to make sure the people they loved were taken care of. I witnessed my grandpa provide, helping people out who should have been providing for themselves.

There is a difference between needing help to get you through a tough situation and simply depending on a person because of consistently making poor decisions. I am sure he looked forward to uneventful glory years, but between the drug dealing, jail sentences, violence, drug use, and death of a few children, I don't see how he and my granny managed to stay sane through it all. I imagine, in some instances in their lives, once they started to get older, they blamed themselves and probably wondered where they went wrong.

I guarantee, somewhere there was a gap, but there are always three sides to a story and there is no manual on how to raise a child properly. Whatever mistakes they made with their own children, my granny and grandpa tried to make it up with their grandchildren. During some of the hardest times our family faced, there was still love among us.

The one thing I remember throughout my entire life when speaking with my dad was him telling me, "Son, never lose your love." I would look at him in amazement, although the message was clear, it was hard for me at times to feel love towards anybody. Some of those discussions came at the most inopportune times, and it was hard for me to take advice from my dad in those situations.

In life, you will struggle with the boundaries of love. I struggled with loving my father at times because of his substance abuse. The hero worship started to fade away over the years. He was the reason I wasn't feeling the love. It's hard to love a person who can change moods at the drop of a dime. He would leave the house in mid-conversation if the right person pulled up in a vehicle. The love that was instilled in me by my mother and father before his addiction helped me through some rough times. In those instances, I had to maintain my love for myself and then for them.

It was hard, but I understood that if I were to disown them and not love them, it would be most detrimental to me. Even though this realization didn't occur to me at the time it was happening, it was my way of preserving myself. If I hate my parents and decide not to honor them, then my self-sabotage was imminent. I maintained my belief that they were trying to do their best for me. I knew my mom was trying her best, but she answered to my dad as head of household. Despite his shortcomings, the one thing he maintained was his love and, although sometimes it was in a backwards way: A way like you can only love a parent, no matter what condition they are in, because you yearn for their love.

In my harsh reality, amidst all the mayhem and chaos which was everyday life for us kids in the inner city, it was evident that a lack of love in a community could ultimately destroy everything you hold dear. Love is presented in several forms, and I am not saying it won't hurt you, but the idea is to harness the power of love in those good times and use it to become free of all the hatred, fear, and pain that tries to manifest itself smothering your internal light. This is a light all human beings were meant to possess, because every one of us has a purpose in this world.

"Our deepest fear is not that we are inadequate. Our deepest fear is that we are powerful beyond measure. It is our light, not our darkness that most frightens us. We ask ourselves, *Who am I to be brilliant, gorgeous, talented, fabulous?* Actually, who are you *not* to be? You are a child of God. Your playing small does not serve the world. There is nothing enlightened about shrinking so that other people won't feel insecure around you. We are all meant to shine, as children do. We were born to make manifest the glory of God that is within us. It's not just in some of us; it's in everyone. And as we let our own light shine, we unconsciously give other people permission to do the same. As we are liberated from our own fear, our presence automatically liberates others."

Marianne Williamson

Allow your light to shine abundantly, do not be afraid to go out and try different things. When I was growing up on the east side of Detroit, it wasn't cool to be a nerd or artistic because you were teased and bullied. I challenge you to go and join the chess club, be artistic, play an instrument, and be the best you can be at it. Love yourself enough to explore the GOD- given talents already bestowed upon you. It's inside of you, waiting to be unleashed on the world.

"If you love what you do, you never work a day in your life" is about earning a living around your dreams and your passions. Focus on the things that you love to create a life of abundance.

Escape Through Following and Leading

To be a great leader, you have to start off as a great follower. Some leaders are born, but the majority are made. Leadership skills are developed through training, experience, and perception. The one thing I learned at an early age—and throughout my life—is to be a leader. If I am not in a position to lead, I need to be a good follower behind a positive and worthy leader.

There are plenty of leaders on both sides of the spectrum: You have leaders that promote negativity and you have those, like me, who want to see people prosper. For instance, Hitler was a "great" leader; he was able to influence millions to get behind his view on the world. He's a terrible example of a leader, but it highlights my point about good and bad leaders. The people who were following Hitler obviously were poor followers. Following the wrong people can ruin your life. It only takes one bad decision. I learned this valuable lesson in middle school.

In the spring of 1992, my parents were preparing to go on another trip to Tennessee as my dad had recently reunited with his estranged father who lived in Nashville. My parents couldn't afford to take all of us on a road trip; there wasn't enough room for my two older brothers and me to make the trip. My parents decided to leave us behind. We were deemed responsible enough to stay at home by ourselves. My dad gave us the whole
 parental speech about making the right decisions, staying out of trouble, etc. once we hugged and kissed our parents goodbye, a feeling of excitement shot through my body. This was my first real experience of freedom as a teenager. Plus, I had my brothers to look after me, so what's the worst that could happen?

The world was at my feet, but of course, the main thing on my mind was to have fun. I didn't have a girlfriend; all the girls I liked in school didn't reciprocate. I didn't have the words to approach a girl. I was the poor kid from the east side, which meant I never had the best clothes or the high-priced gym shoes. The boys that possessed all of the fly gear garnered all of the attention from the girls I liked. So, the alternative—since my parents were out of town—was to hang out and go see all the family members and friends that I was never able to see on a regular basis. It was time to travel around the city and hang out with cousins that I hadn't seen in a while. Most times, my dad forbade us from hanging out with some of our family members, and, honestly looking back, it was for good reason.

Sitting in our second-floor flat, we didn't really know what to do with ourselves without parental supervision. Our father left my brother Ray in charge, his oldest, so we followed his lead. The first idea he had was to break into the flat downstairs. Our neighbors downstairs were a young couple who had two small children. I didn't think it was a good idea, but my oldest brother insisted we go on this heist to get money for our escapade because we weren't left with much. The alarms were ringing inside of me, but I was overruled by my brothers. I felt powerless in the situation.

My experience with anything criminal at this age was zero. The most I had ever done was shoot dice and get into the occasional fight in our neighborhood—usually over a dice game or some form of competitive sport.

Most times my environment dictated how I felt and what my outlook on life was. It was a battle to find a silver lining in my existence every day but, overall, I fought to keep a positive attitude. I battled with the external influences all around me to be a good person. My intentions were not to hurt or take anything from anyone, so breaking into someone's home was never on my list of things to accomplish. I couldn't talk my brothers out of breaking into the downstairs flat, and my only incentive was that I wanted to feel closer to them. Being a little half-brother, I always wanted to be accepted by them. I wanted to be viewed as an equal, one of the guys—which was complex because they had the same mother, and I did not. This created a bit of a divide, a disconnect, and this dynamic made me feel like an outsider in our relationship. At that moment in my life, I was impressionable. I would have done almost anything just to be fully accepted by my brothers. I took brotherhood seriously but often felt the same sentiment was not shared. So, in that moment, seeking acceptance and brotherhood, I made a horrible decision: There was a consensus to move forward with breaking into the downstairs flat. Ray said he would do all the work, he just needed us to watch out. We waited for our neighbors to leave and then our plan went into action. We knew the only way to get into the downstairs flat was through the basement so we opened our back door that led into the basement. As we walked down our steep basement stairs, every step culminated in more fear and nervousness running rampant through my body as sweat collected on my nose. I was apprehensive, but I followed anyway with the hopes of gaining some respect from my brothers and obtaining some money to play arcades at the local liquor store. The basement was divided by a poorly constructed tin metal wall. We peeled back the metal creating an entry point, and we all slipped through to the other side. I was the last through, and my adrenaline was pumping. I'd never done anything like this before, but my brothers seemed like pros. I looked over at Ken, and I could see a little apprehension on his face as we went up the stairs to the back door of the downstairs flat. The old wooden back door with its small pane of glass was all that stood between us and entering the flat. To our surprise, it was unlocked.

We could still turn back and just as I was attempting to say, "Let's not do this..." Ray turned the knob and the door opened easily. Ray stepped from the stairs and into the flat. Ken followed after him. Once I knew the coast was clear, I entered. Ray did not hesitate. He went into the bedroom looking for cash or valuables, and it didn't take long before he discovered a book of food stamps and a little bit of cash. I mainly stayed on the back steps in the doorway waiting, and then I started creeping back to our side of the basement.

My brothers followed behind me soon thereafter, and then we pushed the metal wall back into place to make sure it didn't look like anyone came from our side of the basement. Once back in our flat, we split up whatever food stamps and cash there was which amounted to around a hundred bucks total. Then we hit the streets. The first stop was the corner store where I bought some junk food and traded in some stamps to play arcade games located in the liquor store for a quarter. After, playing games at the store, we caught the bus over to Ray's sister's house. She was older than any of us, and had a car—a grey Dodge Horizon. Somehow Ray was able to get her keys and we took off with the car. Now we had wheels, so we went around the city visiting our cousins and friends. This was one of the closest moments I would have with all three of us being together.

Unfortunately, it was tied to us doing something criminal. After joy riding around the east side of the city, eventually it was time to return the car. She was visibly upset and threatened to tell our dad about our activities in his absence. Our days of hanging out and not having parental supervision were going to end quickly. Since cell phones weren't abundant at the time (only rich people had the resources to have mobile phones in their cars), we had to get home so we could be near the house phone when my dad called. Once on the phone with my dad, we pretended that our time alone was uneventful. The guy downstairs suspected us of breaking into his flat and taking his food stamps, but he couldn't prove it. So, he took it out on his girl. I could hear him going off and putting his hands on her. Maybe my brother Ray was cracking under the pressure of telling his sister where we got the money, or maybe it was the threat that she was going to expose him for taking off with her car, but for some reason, Ray confessed to our dad that we broke into the flat downstairs during this call. I could never figure out why and Ray never explained. The anger in my father's voice was fierce and intimidating after hearing this information. Placing my ear to the receiver and speaking with my father about our escapade would change the way I looked at everything in life from that moment forward. Naturally, my dad was upset and the wrath of his vengeance for our betrayal came down on us through the phone, but it was nothing like what we would soon experience in person.

He was definitely heading back from Tennessee immediately. As we huddled over the phone as he hung up, we were frozen. The anxiety was unbearable waiting for our parents' arrival. I tried to enjoy what little time I had left since, in my mind, death was imminent within 24 to 48 hours. I went over to my best friend's house across the street and shot some hoops, in an effort to keep my mind off what was coming. With every shot, my mind wandered to images of being mangled once my dad got ahold of me.

When my parents finally arrived back home from Tennessee, all hell broke loose. There was a brief discussion, if you can call it that, in which my dad screamed and cussed to no end. My mother simply sat there in disgust. We were surely all "super creeps" to her and the piercing look burned right through the core of my soul. Ray was the first up for a beating because it went from oldest to youngest. It was painful to hear, but we heard everything. Ken and I listened in sheer terror as the beating was laid down on Ray in our shared bedroom. It was ironic that the walls in our room were a bright pink, since hearing my older brother get beat like a runaway slave made me feel like a little girl. I was frightened at what was in store for me. The feelings were mixed for my older brother. During his beating, I was more concerned about myself. How did I allow myself to be manipulated in this way? The words, "Be a Leader" kept ringing out inside my brain. I didn't feel sorry for Ray, why would he dime us out after it was his idea in the first place? The beating was very intense and, after a while, I could hear Ray say, "Kill me"!

A wooden baseball bat always sat faithfully in the corner—to be used for the purposes of protecting our home—but, on this day, my dad picked it up. Just as he was about to bring the bat down on top of my brother's head, my mother was holding onto the other end of it. She saved Ray's life that night. After Ray's beating was done, it was Ken's turn.

During Ken's beating, Ray was balled up next to me in my room like an abused kitten. We listened to Ken scream out into the night, and it was traumatizing. I was next, and the wait was just too much. After Ken came back into the room, his spirit broken, it was my turn to face our father's wrath. I was hoping that my dad would tire out and that my beating wouldn't be so intense, but he was an athletic man and he could be mean as anyone I knew. His stamina was still intact when he saw me. The fury in my dad's eyes and anger in his voice were unmatched by anything I'd ever seen before. The "peace keeper" which was a homemade whip comprised of ironing cords cut to length, was dangling in his hands. He demanded I pull down my pants. He wanted bare rear-ends. Before any whooping, he would always say, "This is going to hurt me more than it's going to hurt you." I always had trouble interpreting that saying. This was not my first encounter with the "peace keeper" but after the first swing, when the ironing cords connected with my naked behind, it broke the silence. The sting and pain was so excruciating, the only thing I could do was fall down and scream, begging for him to stop but that wasn't my dad's style. You were going to take multiple lashes, and if you didn't get up right away you were threatened with a different type of physical harm.

He yelled, "Get your ass up!" I got up with tears in my eyes, and he grabbed the back of my neck to hold me in place, giving me another lash across my behind. I received at least eight more before he was tired enough to allow me to go back into the room with my brothers. It was a long night because, after the beatings, my dad called us back out to speak with him about the situation. The conversation could easily turn into another beating if he felt like you weren't broken or remorseful. If he felt like you didn't understand, he would beat you again.

Our screams and cries echoed throughout the neighborhood that night as the "peace keeper" connected to our raw behinds. The beatings were bad, but what hurt the most was that I let my parents down. It was shameful and stupid, and I'd followed my way right into some major trouble. That was one of the worst beatings in my life, but it taught me a lesson: At any point in your life, don't follow an individual who is not about the right thing. Do not follow a person who is unfit to lead you in a positive direction.

After a night of horror, all three of us were whimpering and licking our wounds in the pink room. After a while, we were allowed to lay down for bed. Unfortunately, that was not the end to our sorrows. The next day my older brother moved out of the house. Ken and I were put to work as part of our punishment. We had to dig up a plot of land next door where a house once stood. We were working hard, digging into hard dirt with dull shovels. I had to jump with an unsurmountable amount of force on top of that shovel to break into that dirt. Blisters started forming on the inside of my hands, especially the outer skin on my thumb. When Ray came out of the house with a bag full of his belongings, we stopped to bid him farewell.

During our "goodbyes," I was thinking about how he really screwed us over. There was an opportunity for him to pick up a shovel and help his little brothers but instead he waved goodbye and went on his way. A disdain for our older brother was born that day, and it created a permanent rift in our relationship-—brotherhood would never be the same. The weeks that followed were filled with hard stares of disappointment and disgust from our parents. Ken and I suffered the entire summer. It was nothing but hard work for summer vacation, no playing, laughing or joking in an environment that was already unpleasant. But, I always told myself things could always get worse.

I share this story as an example of how one bad decision can alter your life. We disrupted a family and caused strife in someone else's relationship. We were lucky to walk away with only bruised butts and temporarily broken spirits. Our parents weren't raising us to behave this way. They were trying to keep us out of jail and out of the cemetery. The first time we were left home alone for a few days, we betrayed our parents' trust. During that time in my life doing something of that nature never crossed my mind, but I was persuaded by my need for acceptance. My desire for acceptance from my older brothers was so strong it propelled me, against by better judgment, to follow them into a terrible situation.

This is why you must always follow the right people. You must surround yourself with people who want to keep you out of harm's way, people who care about your well-being. In my situation, I should have stayed behind, on my side of the basement. In life, especially in an environment that is filled with inadequacies, low self-esteem, and hopelessness, we tend to gravitate toward people who seem to know what to do in these negative situations. Most times people are leading you incorrectly because they've never been taught how to do things right themselves. When someone wants to lead you down a path of destruction, step up and lead yourself. Explain why it's a bad idea and provide all the reasons why you shouldn't make a bad decision. It only takes one bad decision to put you behind bars or in a cemetery.

Escape Through Positive Relationships

It is important to keep positive people around you. Have you ever heard the quote, "Don't spend major time with minor people"? This quote is not to belittle or marginalize those who can't do better, but instead signifies that a person has the ability to surround himself with people who want more out of life.

A person's destiny can be positive or negative, but it depends on the type of energy you allow into your life. When I was younger, my family was close and I had male cousins who I loved. I wanted to hang out with them every chance I got. My dad would limit my exposure to my cousins because they were a couple years older than me and stayed in trouble. My cousins weren't serious about their education and they were headed down the wrong path. How could you blame them? All of our role models were involved in criminal activities. There was a normalcy to crime in my neighborhood. Our environment was criminal, plain and simple. It didn't care whether you were smart or if you had a future... if you weren't careful it would swallow you whole, chew you up, and spit out the remains of your maimed corpse for your mother to cry over.

The problem during that time was that my cousins had decided to start selling drugs. Thinking back, it's crazy to visualize middle-school-age children selling drugs to adults. Where would they even get the drugs to sell? Well, you had adults giving it to children on consignment to sell. How do you escape a place that is so negative that adults are leading their children down the wrong path? Anyone who gives you drugs to sell is not a friend of yours. There are better ways in life to make money. It's a road that will lead to jail or death, and other unimaginable things because, believe it or not, there are things worse than jail or death. It's a proven path. This is not a theory you need to test. There is no easy solution but you need to always surround yourself with positive people.

Everyone should be working toward a positive goal, no matter what their circumstances may be. If you find some majorly positive people to help you along your journey, it becomes much easier. Life becomes easier when you can share experiences and lessons learned with others, harnessing those experiences to further one another along in life's journey. If one individual in your group hits a rough patch or roadblock in life, there is no reason why the rest of your group should experience the same pitfall. The key is to ensure that corrective actions are in place for the next phase of the journey, and this can be accomplished through brainstorming to solve problems together.

The need for positive role models is enormous, especially in impoverished areas. If all you see on the news is robbery and murder, and then once you walk outside, your neighborhood is nothing but dilapidated buildings, drug addicts, dealers, and violence, it becomes very difficult to differentiate these things from your own life. It becomes difficult to determine who the real cool people are in your community, and whom you should avoid at all costs.

Although it couldn't be helped because of my environment, my parents tried their best to limit exposure to bad influences. Unfortunately, enough bad influence was under our own roof. I feared my dad. He lived by the mantra, "Do as I say not as I do". That was enough for me because he didn't play when it came to following orders. Being unable to hang with my cousins, friends, or brothers whenever I wanted was painful growing up. But they always seemed to be in some kind of trouble.

The aunts and uncles on my mother's side who were college graduates exposed me to a very different way of life. Spending time with family members with a different approach and perspective on life provided a much needed alternative and calm to my young, impressionable life. When I visited my maternal grandmother, I would see an entirely different way of living. She stayed on the west side of town, which was much nicer than where we lived. It was a different atmosphere, and although no one was rich and there were still dangers, there was less gunfire and the burned-out structures were minimal. I could actually walk to the store with my grandmother and have very little fear of something bad happening.

If you live in a bad part of town, try to get some exposure outside of your area. There is a whole world out there, and you have to go see it. Be adventurous! Having the ability to visit another side of town and see people with a slightly different mindset had a big influence on what I wanted for myself and it will do the same for you. If you want to escape the pitfalls, you have to do things that may not be conventional for the rest of your family or friends. For those who have an outlet and an opportunity to experience something different, take that time to reflect on what life could be, and envision yourself being successful. It's okay to go see family members out in the suburbs even if your immediate family thinks it's crazy. Go spend time with that aunt or uncle. Learn all you can because there are kin folk who can offer you insights that those closest to you cannot.

Parents, make sure your child is always exposed to positive men and women. Whether this is in your church, within your family, or at your job, it doesn't matter; having a mentor is one of the keys to success. During my visits to the west side, my mother's brother would come and take me to the movies. His kindness and love was evident because my uncle was spending time with me, and those bus rides to the theater were priceless to me. They allowed me to develop a love and kindness in my own heart. Ultimately, my uncle's kindness helped me be a better brother, father, husband, son, and uncle. A trickle-down effect happens when you instill love and positivity. It can change the dynamics of your family, the community, and the world. GOD placed you on this planet to fulfill a destiny.

One person who undoubtedly accomplished a lot during his short life is my all-time favorite rapper, Tupac Shakur. Our beloved artist, who touched so many hearts, was speaking up for people who didn't have a voice. He frequently used his platform as a megastar to highlight the injustices of people who are less fortunate and those oppressed by the system. Tupac didn't have to speak up for his people but he risked everything to speak out. Tupac was a revolutionary beyond his time. When I listened to his music it resonated with me. I originally heard his song "Brenda's Got a Baby" through a music video show on cable. The song was so powerful because I saw Brenda in my neighborhood, in my loved-ones. People who were used and abused. The song was about a twelve-year-old girl who was nothing more than a means for her mother to receive a welfare check. She was a girl who was not loved, unimportant to the people who were supposed to care for her. Tupac wrote his verses so descriptively, and his lyrics were matched with powerful visuals in his music video.

The song was important; too many young people have stories that are similar—even identical—to Brenda's. I will never forget the melodic tune or Tupac rapping his lyrics in "Brenda's Got a Baby." Tupac saved my life with his lyrics. When Tupac spoke in interviews and performed, I felt like he was talking directly to me. That's how I was able to get through some of my own hardships.

Unfortunately, I can also use my favorite rapper in several examples of how having the wrong relationships and energy becomes unproductive and lethal. Tupac was accused of rape in 1994. I believe one of the key reasons Tupac was placed in a position to be accused of such a heinous crime is because there was negative energy and people who were not conducive to his well-being. The only people who know exactly what happened that night are those who were involved.

While fighting rape allegations, he was shot five times while being robbed. All of his fans were glad he survived the robbery but in disbelief over everything their favorite artist was experiencing. It's the same premise, when you associate with people who are in the streets with bad intentions: Eventually it will impact your life in a negative way. Shortly after being shot, he was convicted of a lesser charge and sentenced to eighteen-to- fifty-four months in prison. Tupac, arguably, the most prolific and genius rap artist of our time had his life cut short prematurely not even nineteen months after being sentenced. Over the years there have been plenty of barbershop arguments, documentaries, celebrity and non-celebrity interviews on how Tupac came to his demise on that horrible night in Las Vegas, Nevada.

There were plenty of probable causes leading to Tupac's demise, and the big fight at the Las Vegas casino could be identified as the specific cause. He was signed to a record company with gang ties in Los Angeles. Granted, he signed with Death Row records to get released from prison which was the consequence of negative people and energy from the rape case in New York. Once with Death Row records his attitude changed, and although we loved his music, charisma, and persona, he was influenced by negativity which changed his public persona. He was not a gangster, but he kept company with individuals who were living that lifestyle. These people didn't possess his talent and intellect, but they vowed to protect him. I am sure he wanted to reciprocate these sentiments to his friends. The truth is, they couldn't protect him because there is no defense from a person's own internal struggles. When you are young, the feeling of invincibility is inherent, and although you see people's lives changing around you, there is still a thought that these life-changing scenarios won't befall you. I am here to tell you, they will. Nobody is exempt from something terrible happening. The key is to mitigate the risk of these critical events.

From a public eye, it appeared Tupac took on a new persona. Nobody could be sure how he really felt inside. Only GOD knows the answer. Tupac's new persona was one I didn't recognize, but still revered. In that short time, it seems there was no escape from the negative influence. How could someone so positive become so outwardly negative in their approach to people and an entire industry? I suppose, it was a culmination of the trauma experienced in such short amount of time. It was enough drama to drive anyone down a path of rage and mistrust. Nonetheless, the negativity killed him. Some people may blame his demise on signing with

Death Row and being affiliated with gang members. If you dig deeper into Tupac's life— truly conducting a root cause analysis—it all relates back to that fateful night in New York in Tupac's hotel room. The events that transpired forced a young lady to file rape charges against Tupac and his associates. Think about it: If that night in New York never happens, Tupac doesn't go to jail; this keeps him free, so he never needs to sign a deal with Death Row Records who had known gang affiliations. Of course, I cannot say definitively that Tupac would still be alive if New York never happened. He had already been shot without Death Row in his life but I believe Tupac's risks would have been mitigated. If Tupac doesn't get into trouble and sent to prison, there's a great chance Tupac would have been able to live a lot longer, perhaps even being here with us today.

I used Tupac's life events because, it's a perfect example of how negative relationships can and will destroy everything. It also shows how events and people are interrelated and how there is always a cause and effect in life. Bad decisions made today can affect your life years later. Stay away from bad people and decisions. If you have a misstep or make a bad decision, implement a permanent corrective action so it won't reoccur. I want you to live a full life. There is no honor in dying young or going to prison so you can be locked away like an animal. There is purpose for you in this world, and entertaining positive people will propel you to unimaginable heights.

One night, I was hanging out with my older cousins, and on our way to my aunt's house which was several blocks away, we made a couple of stops to sell drugs they acquired. As a twelve-year-old kid, I was just happy my parents let me hang with them on this particular night. I looked up to my older cousins. It was all about getting into the streets and seeing how much fun we could have. We were young and totally aware of all the possibilities and dangers that were lurking in the night. I was a typical kid pushing the boundaries. My parents didn't have accurate knowledge of my whereabouts, of course. I was supposed to be spending the night at my aunt's, but during our commute, we took the scenic route.

This particular night was different and taught me a lesson about having the right energy around me know matter the sacrifice. Building positive relationships will require sacrifice. Committing to positive relationships will eliminate some family and friends from your life. Be prepared to have lonely days, you are worth the sacrifice. In my case, I knew drugs were being sold, guns were being toted, and it didn't trigger an alarm for me. Part of me wanted to be down with my cousins, and although I wasn't handling the drugs, we were all together and I had a choice to go back home. During this night, we were eventually split up, and two of my cousins went on another mission and I was left with my favorite cousin. Still, deep down inside my conscious, my inner voice was saying, *What are you doing? Go home. Get out of these streets.*

We went to his house first to see what was going on over there, and it was the same old thing. My aunt had people in and out of the house, mainly staying in the upstairs bedroom getting high. There was no time for us, so we were disregarded. We took off to my house which was around the corner. We started walking down a side street and once we crossed over Lakewood on Forest, my cousin said, "You always have to watch yourself out here. Like this guy on the bike behind us..." Before he mentioned this person, I didn't hear anybody, but when I looked back there was a guy on a ten-speed bike, half a block away from us. My cousin calmly said, "Once we cross this street, start jogging." Respecting his street knowledge, I listened to him, startled and confused, we started jogging across the street. The man started to speed up on his bike, then he pulled a yellow ski mask over his face and said, "Don't run now. I got you." As he said that, he sped up on his bike and he pulled out a big automatic pistol. At that moment, time stood still! I felt helpless. Was this my time to die?

The gunman pointed and shot directly at us. The entire moment seemed to be in slow motion. I saw muzzle flashes from the gun which lit up the darkness like fireworks on a night in July. In that moment, I had to make a split decision: Either run with my cousin or split off by myself. If I run with my cousin, there was a greater chance of getting shot because the shooter was positioned in the street, right in middle of us. GOD gave me the right decision-making skills that night. After the initial shots rang out, I took off running the opposite way my cousin chose. I looked back just to see my cousin turning a corner—we probably turned our respective corners at the same time—and I bolted up a neighbor's driveway into their backyard, jumping the fence and snagging my favorite pair of Bugle Boy cargo pants. I landed in an alley on the other side and had to jump another fence into an adjacent backyard. From there, I ran down another driveway and across the street to my aunt's house. Out of breath and frantic, I banged on the door. After minutes that seemed like hours, my aunt came down from her upstairs bedroom and let me in. I immediately gathered myself and explained what had just happened. "Aunty, we were just shot at by a guy on a bike!" I shouted this at her, barely able to get it out due to shortness of breath from running like Carl Lewis during the 100- meter dash.

Thankfully neither one of us was shot that night but using this example helps to describe why I want you to surround yourself with positive people and energy. Surrounding myself with negative people—although they are loved ones—almost cost me my life.

I am not here to say that all these principles of positivity are 100-percent effective but if you use them to view the world differently, it can save you plenty of mistakes and heartache, and it may just save your life. I was influenced by negativity and I picked up tendencies that were not conducive to success. This seemed inevitable because of my surroundings, but as I got older I met more like-minded people who were going through the same struggles, and this was helpful in trying to find a way out of the self-destructive path I was on.

Escape Through Inner Strength

Finding inner strength is easier said than done. The strength you require lies in believing in a higher power. Every man, woman, and child need to believe in something greater than themselves. I don't care who you consider GOD. It can be Allah, Jesus, Jehovah, Buddha—it doesn't matter.

To quote the late great Muhammad Ali, "There is good in every religion."

I tend to agree with Muhammad Ali. As you journey through life, especially if you have encountered multiple changes introduced by a toxic environment, you will need to go deep down within your soul to survive. Prayer is a great way to get through those dark times, but they must be followed with action. GOD will listen to your prayer but typically a miracle is not performed right at the moment of request. But, if action is placed behind that prayer, the odds of something good happening are greater for tomorrow, next week, or next year depending on your circumstance.

There are times where a miracle won't happen at all. These times will leave you questioning everything—even your faith in a higher power. Trust me I've been there. I wondered where GOD was during some of the times I was suffering, but I would quickly correct myself and lean on GOD even more in my times of despair. Now, reflecting on my upbringing and everything I made it through, I realize that GOD was with me the entire time.

In these times, you must not falter in your faith. You must believe that everything happens for a reason. The reason for the absence of a miracle may be designed to strengthen or teach a hard lesson in that particular moment. Inner strength is built during those tough times in life: the passing of a loved one, losing someone to the prison system unexpectedly. Inner strength has to be built on love for yourself and an unshakable belief system. When things happen that are meant to derail your life, you must rely on the love for yourself to be at the core of decision making. Inner strength encompasses so many different variables. There may be several events in your life that make you want to quit, but during that time you must rely on the love for yourself and fight to live.

When you are faced with circumstances that can place you in jail and away from your loved ones, inner strength and love for one's self must deter you from making a critical mistake. I never understood why so many people allow a small situation to turn into a larger one. In these moments, you must rely on inner strength and self-love to keep yourself safe. Once inner strength is harnessed, no one can deter you from greatness because—like Muhammad Ali—you begin to build yourself physically, emotionally, and mentally.

I will never forget one of the things the late, great

Muhammad Ali said in one of his interviews. He said that when he works out in anticipation of a fight, he doesn't count his reps during workout because it doesn't count until he is tired. My dad would always tell me the fight doesn't start until you are tired. I often wonder if he got that from Muhammad Ali, but either way they are both right and these are words to live by. The fight for your mind, body, and soul doesn't start until you are tired. During this weariness, you will *have to* fight.

Love for yourself will make you feel like you're worth it. If you're backed by the inner strength you've been exercising, you will be well prepared for what the world has in store for you. Inner strength is your mind, body, and soul harnessing a higher power that to assist with persevering through hard times. During the times that are toughest, close your eyes and ask GOD to bring you through your situation. In the words of Tupac Shakur, "If you can make it through the night, there is a brighter day." This is one of my all-time favorite lines, and I've used his words to get me through plenty of hard days and nights. Speak the words but always put action behind them. There was never a time I said a prayer and didn't put action behind them to improve my life.

The only way to improve your life is to focus on a goal and keep putting a string of successful days together. These successful days, will turn into successful weeks, months and years. Today, as I look at my children experience all the things I was unable to do, I can't help but to think about what my life would be like if I had given up on myself and GOD so many years ago. Would I even be here? What if I had taken my life because the inner strength required to survive was never developed? I would have missed out on all these blessings. Inner strength can be difficult because it requires so much discipline. It consists of many virtues that must be mastered over time. I use inner strength in times when it's much easier to use violence to express myself. In these times, it requires a certain discipline and inner strength to walk away from someone who has wronged me. But, I remember that one simple act of aggression can alter my life tremendously.

It doesn't matter what nationality, race, religion, or walk of life you come from. The one thing that is certain is you will face adversity. The type of adversity experienced will surely differ between individuals and groups but the ability to handle these issues when faced with them will determine how you move through life. Do this properly—with positivity—and you will overcome whatever type of adversity you are faced with in life.

Like my neighborhood growing up, yours may be infested with drug use and violence. In these cases, the negativity will act as a fog, reducing your visibility and ability to navigate to a higher level. In these instances, I was able to build inner strength. I want you to do the same. Make a commitment to yourself that you will not become another statistic.

Growing up as a black male in Detroit I faced much adversity: food shortage in the house, utilities being shut off, drug-addicted family members, violence, I had to find a way to confront these situations and survive. I started to develop an inner strength, which allowed me to bend my circumstances to my will. In the movie "*The Hurricane*", Denzel Washington stars as a boxer from Patterson, New Jersey who is wrongfully convicted of a triple homicide. The film is based on the true story of light heavyweight boxing champ Rubin Carter. The film is set in 1960s when black people were dealing with civil rights injustices daily, so a black man being wrongfully accused for crimes they didn't commit was the norm. Once in prison, Denzel portrayed Rubin Carter as a man who was resilient, a fighter whose pedigree was undeniable.

He would not admit to a crime he did not commit. There is a scene from this movie that resonates with me and my own internal battles with life. Because he was incarcerated as an innocent man, he would face his adversity by making himself stronger mentally and physically. Rubin vowed that the system would not break him. He would control what he could. Rubin would exact power over his situation, even under prison rules. In the movie, he decided to turn his body into a weapon, become a gladiator through his adversity, and strengthen his mental capacity. He would sleep when the other prisoners were awake. He would not eat their food. This reminds me of how I became my own kind of gladiator as a young man.

Although Rubin Carter had to spend years in prison, and he needed to build up a toughness to survive his long unfortunate stay there, love and persistence is ultimately what freed him. In the movie, a young man reads about Rubin's story and is able to convince some close relatives and friends to help look at Rubin's case. This, ultimately, sets in motion the plan to get him out of prison.

All of the principles in this book help you to face adversity. There are going to be some things that happen in your life that are out of your control. Nobody can predict what events and circumstances will present themselves in the future, but you have to elevate yourself, build inner strength, and take on adversity with a positive attitude. If you do this, I guarantee you can turn a bad situation into one that can help catapult your life in the right direction. All my life, I felt there was a black cloud over my head. There were no easy breaks for me, even though everyone else seemed to get them—even those who were not good people. I stopped throwing myself a pity party and started to live by these principles I've outlined in this book. When I did that, things started to look up for me.

Escape Through Elevation

The journey will not be easy, but if you stay true to the art of elevation, the reward will be much greater because you will avoid pitfalls that can derail your success. There were plenty of times when I wanted to use violence to resolve issues and, in some cases, I used my fist to handle it. During my years in elementary and middle school when I had issues in my neighborhood they were settled with fights. If the problem came to me, I didn't turn the other cheek. In my environment, using violence to solve issues was a learned behavior. This method of problem solving was not necessarily promoted by my parents, but it wasn't frowned upon either. Besides, I saw violence right outside my door all the time which served as a constant example for the younger generation in the neighborhood. People weren't living by the philosophy of Gandhi or Martin Luther King Jr. Peace wasn't being preached, and if you tried the non-violent route it would end badly for you. We simply grew up believing most confrontations should be resolved with force.

I was no troublemaker growing up, but sometimes you couldn't escape situations, and that's when you had to defend yourself. If trouble finds you, use your brain to figure out a way to avoid the situation. You can't always see those issues coming either. The key is to mitigate your risk of being involved in a situation that may present a violent or unnecessary scenario. Trust me, I know about situations that can't be avoided—but when you can, you avoid them or elevate above them.

 During ninth grade at Martin Luther King high school, trouble found me on the Jefferson bus route which was headed to downtown Detroit. After school one day, I was traveling to an area called the "north end" to play basketball where my father worked at Considine recreation center. The Detroit bussing system was filled with risk because there were kids from other schools who weren't about the right thing and adults who posed a threat as well. I didn't know much about the area, and I didn't know many people in that neighborhood.

I transferred to Martin Luther King High from Finney High which was nine miles away. I didn't have the backup of my siblings or cousins to keep me safe. I was like a fish out of water, but there were two freshmen students I'd met who I befriended in the first couple months of being at King High. There was a Job Corp. campus further east of where King students got on the bus. Job Corp had programs for kids who were out of high school and looking to pick up a skilled trade. The young men who went to Job Corp. had a reputation for being troublemakers. That day when I stepped onto the bus with my two fellow ninth graders, I learned a very valuable lesson.

The bus was very crowded. It had orange hard plastic seats, but it didn't matter because there was nowhere to sit anyway, so me and my buddies made our way to the back where we had to stand up. It was winter, so I had a thick puffy coat on with my hood drawn so tight, my vision was impaired. I could barely carry my backpack and maneuver through the bus passengers. Unfortunately, the Job Corp. teens were known for bothering younger kids from King or whoever else they could harass because they were older and could bully the younger, less-experienced students. They also knew a good percentage of the kids that went to King didn't have much experience with the streets. There were a handful, of course, but King was one of the better schools in the city—both academically and geographically—so if your parents looked to get you in that school someone was trying to help you elevate. The same didn't apply to other students in the city and on this day, it definitely didn't apply to these guys on the bus.

My friends and I weren't on the bus for three stops before a guy sitting in a seat told my friend Kevin he had to move because he couldn't see his boy on the other side of him. Kevin ignored him the first time and then the guy said it again with more conviction. In that moment, I wanted Kevin to elevate and just try to move out of the guy's way, make a compromise because I knew we were outnumbered. The guy said, "You better move out the way." I still hear Kevin's words clearly as if it was yesterday. Kevin told the guy, "You haven't said nothing but a word." In my head, I was mortified. I was out of my element, so far from home and I knew we were surrounded on this crowded bus that smelled of diesel fuel and exhaust.

Two guys with something to prove jumped up simultaneously and hit Kevin. In fear, I managed to move forward to help Kevin but with a 20-to-30-pound book bag on my back and low visibility, a guy jumped up in front of me and said, "What are you going to do" before hitting me square in my mouth. If the bus wasn't crowded, it would have probably knocked me down but instead I stumbled back onto our other friend who was behind me. As I was about to lunge back, LeCarl grabbed me and began pulling me off the bus. All I could see was the Job Corp. folks standing up saying something I couldn't quite make out.

I could feel my lips swelling and my bottom two teeth were slightly chipped. I spit out very tiny pieces of enamel as we exited the bus. When the bus rolled off, I realized that Kevin stayed on it. I was scared for him. What was that group of guys going to do to him once they got downtown? There wasn't much to say to Carl at this point, but I told him that I was going to head back to the east side. We parted ways and I caught the bus toward home. There were some people from my school onboard and I explained to them what happened as I covered my mouth. Once I got home, I called my dad and told him the story. Both of my parents were upset, but these were the problems we faced living in the inner city.

Once I settled in that evening, I kept trying to call Kevin but there was no answer. I was really worried because I had no idea what happened to him once he got off the bus downtown. Eventually, he answered and told me he was fine. They did take his skull cap though, and I am sure his ears were cold on the way home. I was just happy he was okay.

The bus situation was a big test for me because when I looked in the mirror and saw that my lips were double the size they should be, it made me very angry. I really wanted to hurt the guy that punched me in the mouth. My mind was briefly wrapped around the idea of exacting revenge. I had options for violence. I could retaliate and have those people hurt just like me. My target would have been anyone at Job Corp. because I couldn't remember the guy's face. Everything had happened so fast, and again my vision was impaired by my hood. My access to weapons was not a problem. There were always guns available, and I envisioned a scenario where I rolled by and shot up their campus on Jefferson, letting them feel the pain and embarrassment I felt. I had family and friends asking me how I wanted to handle the situation. Classmates were calling my house saying how "messed up" it was and asking, "You wanna go up there to Job Corp.?" The kids who were calling had access to guns as well. The unfortunate problem is we could find a gun faster than something to eat. There I was sitting in my room, a 13-year-old kid actually thinking about causing harm to someone or even death because of a punch to my face.

In that instance, I thought about what violence had *really* solved in my short life. I realized it never resolved anything because violence begets more violence. I thought about my uncles who had been murdered and the countless young men in my position that made the wrong decision in this moment and were sitting in juvenile facilities waiting to turn twenty-one, just to be shipped to an adult prison for the rest of their lives. In those thoughts, everything began to become so clear: I got punched in the mouth. I was still alive and there are worse things in this world. My swollen lips eventually went down, sinful pride and ego would heal. I decided to elevate above the situation. I wasn't about to give up my life because someone else had chosen to take a wrong turn in their life.

Once I elevated my thought process, I knew my decision

was the right one. I couldn't throw my life away. Yes, it was embarrassing to be victimized in that way, but I decided to learn from the incident and never allowed someone to make me a victim again. I took a couple days off from school and healed. Once I came back there was a lot of love from fellow students in the hallways. I elevated above those older guys who assaulted me, and I felt relieved. I was onto something. I still had my life, my hopes and dreams, and I was not going to be derailed by foolish emotions in the moment. I thought about every possible scenario and their consequences. I wasn't going to let some knuckleheads take my dream away from me. In my eyes, I had already made it through too much to turn back or let go. From this incident, I became even smarter about how I navigated the streets. I changed my route. I didn't take the Jefferson downtown anymore, not because I was scared, but because it was smart. I took the route where the majority of kids from my school took. If I kept running into people that wanted to harm me, there would have been a bad outcome. I never wanted to risk myself or my family for anything involving me, so I mitigated risk for everyone.

Try elevating in every situation. Try it out with a sibling or a friend. When someone makes you mad, be the bigger person in the situation. If there are troublemakers at your school or at your job, keep your distance if at all possible. Once you start elevating in this way, people will constantly try to derail your progress. But, you must stay the course and fulfill your destiny.

There are plenty of people who didn't learn how to elevate in situations that could have easily been avoided. Instead they chose to play on the same level as someone who didn't deserve any engagement and it cost them their freedom, opportunities, and possibly their lives. Train your mind to identify these situations, and to think about all possibilities and consequences of your actions.

I had mutual friends of a young man who went to a suburban high school outside of Detroit. He had an issue with a classmate and instead of elevating, he engaged his fellow student, punching him in the face. The kid fell back, hitting his head on the concrete. The impact of the fall on the kids head placed him into a coma. The young mans family had to keep him on life support for years. The classmate who struck him, turned into a young adult with this situation looming over him. I am sure, he felt horrible about what happened. He was also terrified because if that kid, who at the time was also a young adult died, he would be charged with his death. Well, after years of being on life support and countless news stories, the bed ridden kid passed away. This meant the young man would now be charged with manslaughter. By this time, he had a wife and child of his own. Unfortunately, he and his family were left to deal with the consequences of a decision made as a teenager.

Can you picture yourself moving on in life, without knowing if you would be able to outpace a bad decision you once made years ago? It's not a pleasant situation, and I'm sure it will affect other decisions and circumstances in your life. I am sure there was a group of people who condemned this young man over a high school fight—something so trivial. But, this happens all the time. We see all the videos of people duking it out on social media, but what people never grasp is there are always consequences to poor decisions (some more severe than others).

The key is to elevate and avoid situations like this. Once these horrible scenarios unfold, there is no turning back. In this story, the man ended up getting convicted of manslaughter and sentenced to prison time. He had to spend significant time away from his family. Once you are locked away, the world does not stop. I've witnessed people get imprisoned and have to miss births, weddings, deaths, everything because of a poor decision. These scenarios will present themselves to you throughout life, and you must elevate above them.

I made elevating a part of my thought process: Never let someone else put you in a compromising situation that can stop your life, hopes, and dreams. If logic and reasoning is used in every situation, you will be able to elevate over people who don't have that ability. When I talk about elevating to a higher level, I am not saying that you are better than the next person, but if someone is behaving in a way that could be detrimental to your health, exit immediately. Too many times, people fail to leave a bad situation, whether it's a fight or the precursor to criminal activity. Too many times, people don't want to look uncool or they are afraid of what others will think.

When you elevate, it's about making the decision and committing to yourself that being a success in life is more important than seeming cool to a person that doesn't matter in the big picture. People have made the mistake of trying to be perceived a certain way or trying to impress someone who doesn't really care about their well-being. Don't make this mistake!

One evening, I was watching an interview with well-known hip-hop artist Kevin Gates. Kevin is not short on trials and tribulations in his life—like most of us who come from these forgotten boroughs and cities. Although Kevin has been riddled with legal problems and questionable decision making, you can learn from anyone. Based on an interview I was watching on the Breakfast Club, a popular Hip-Hop morning show, Kevin has been through a lot in his life, but he's a very articulate young man who spoke about how he and his wife travel together for shows and other business activities without an entourage or bodyguards. He stated that if he had to defend them he could, but he also avoids ignorant people; he simply goes the other way. He refuses to engage that person. The message I took from his interview was to avoid and elevate over individuals who looking to engage in negative behavior. Don't engage those people who want to stop your progress. Thanks Kevin that will forever be a part of everyone's thought process when we are confronted with ignorance.

When you go on your positive journey, there will be

plenty of people put in place as roadblocks to stall and deter you from traveling down your road of success. Remember, you must not engage, you must elevate. Elevation is a principle which must be practiced throughout life's journey because even when you make it out, some of the roadblocks will get higher and wider. The more success you have in life, the more people and situations will try to derail you. The higher you are, the further you can fall. If you've worked hard to get yourself out, never let anyone put you back inside that box. There are examples of successful people all around us who came out of dire situations, but still carry scars that can bring them down if they are not careful. Once you escape, continue to elevate to greater heights. Continue to utilize all the principles outlined in this book. To quote Michelle Obama, "When they go low, you go high."

I'll say it again: In order to escape dire situations life presents during critical moments, you must elevate mind, body, and spirit to a higher level. Logic and reasoning must be a part of every thought process. Every thought before an action should be assessed and a true understanding of consequences from said actions should be properly visualized. If that action or situation will put you in jail, cause harm to anyone—especially someone you love—exit that scenario immediately. Sometimes there will be situations you can't avoid, but minimizing the risk and negative exposure to your life is your responsibility. The way to achieve this is simple: Stay away from situations that are negative. If you can't stay away from it because the negative person is in your household or if your neighborhood is infested with drug use and violence, start to build inner strength and commit to yourself that you will not become another statistic. If there are any programs in your area where you can spend most of your time reading, studying, exercising, it is imperative that you seek them out. Request information from a student counselor at school but you must grow up and commit to yourself. The journey will not be easy, but the reward will be much greater.

Escape Through Letting Go

It's alright to reflect on your past, but do not live in it—especially if it is a history filled with pain and letdowns. Always look to move forward in life, leave the past behind you. If your past was great, it's all good. Continue to create more achievements and memories you can build on, and you will receive an abundance of positivity into your life. If this is the case, be grateful that your past was not filled with negativity. If you are still in a good place, look to pull someone up with you who wants to create new and fulfilling memories.

I've witnessed individuals live in the past totally sabotaging any chance of growth or opportunity because they couldn't let go of certain situations. Don't allow past issues to destroy your future. Listen, I am not saying that past issues just go away. I struggled with letting go of the past. I was always wondering what my life would be like if some of the adults in my life stepped up one-hundred percent. What if I didn't grow up in an impoverished, drug-infested neighborhood? What if I didn't have to grow up through all the pain and suffering of having a parent on drugs? What if my uncles were doctors and lawyers instead of street guys who would be murdered, leaving me and the family unprotected? These are questions I asked consistently throughout my early life when I was in a tight spot.

I was asking questions because I needed answers; I needed help to understand why there was no one to assist me with the right advice or guidance when I needed it or when I was having a hard time financially. In those times, I wanted to give up but I kept moving forward. Living in a negative past will dissolve everything you hold near and dear. Living in the past will prevent any clear vision into your illustrious future. Remember that greatness is truly intended for your life.

When I started being transparent about my life, it was uncomfortable in the beginning. Most of my friends were from different situations and couldn't believe some of the things that I'd experienced in such a short time. But, I started feeling better about myself after sharing my stories, because in talking to people, I also realized my plight was not isolated. Everyone had things they overcame and things they were still working to defeat. This gave me a sense of relief because the mask was removed. My close friends knew what I was going through and they used what wisdom they had to help me get over my issues. Do not be afraid to share your past with a close friend who you trust, or a counselor who is trained to assist people in crisis. If you look to speak with people who can help you about your past or current situation, you will see that you are not alone and there are so many people in this world willing to help you be successful. This makes you stronger. Sometimes we need to get out of our own way. This will not be easy, but you must make it a point to forgive the wrongs of your past and move forward. Eventually, I came to the conclusion that I could no longer blame my stagnation on my past or the inability of others to do right by me. I had to be accountable for myself. I let go of my negative past to the best of my ability and created the life I wanted, you can do the same. Constantly seek ways to further yourself in positivity.

Escape Through Responsibility and Accountability

I remember being in college and not knowing where my next meal would come from. My whole entire life had been a struggle and I was getting frustrated in these times. There were so many times I wanted to give up because of my circumstances. Although I had people around me, I felt alone because my situation was different. The one thing my dad was never short on was words of wisdom and love. So, even though he didn't support me financially, he would talk me off the ledge. He would help me to keep my eyes on the prize. It took a lot of maturity on my part to accept his wisdom and love in that way because I could easily blame him for all of my misfortunes and financial strife, too. It was a very complex relationship because I loved and hated him at the same time. I didn't want to hear words of wisdom in those moments. I wanted to hear, "Son, I am going to send you some money so you can pay rent, get books, or eat." Those words never came out of his mouth, but I always found a way to make it by the grace of GOD.

I had friends and other family members who assisted me throughout my journey. Everyone will have those situations where someone is not doing what they need to do to support you or maybe your expectations are not being met. As human beings, who are flawed, we often believe there should be more that people do for us. The truth is, having expectations for some people is not a smart strategy, especially when they have a proven record of letting you down. Once you get to high school it's time to take responsibility for your own life without expecting anything from anyone else. Stay focused on your goals and leave the negative past behind you. The questions in your head may be like mine (or quite different), but the key is to never let these thoughts find a home in your mental and emotional space. I would go through a bevy of emotions as a teenager, mainly because I had no one to discuss my problems with. When I was growing up, we didn't have the Internet, social media, or any platform to discuss problems openly and publicly. We grew up in an era where you kept your mouth shut and didn't discuss what went on in your household or family business. I had to keep a lot of emotions and pain bottled up inside throughout my childhood to adulthood.

College was where I started taking more control over my life and realizing that someone else's problems and actions didn't make me less of a person. In my case, there is a sense of embarrassment that comes with being one of the "Have Nots." You might feel the same way. But don't feel sorry for yourself. Maybe having a parent that has a substance abuse problem or coming from a single-family household is detrimental, but you have to see a light at the end of the tunnel.

When you are young, there will always be embarrassing moments and situations. Don't dwell on them. Take these times in stride and learn from them. Once I started telling myself that no one could embarrass me, I felt more confident about my struggles and mistakes because we are all just trying to figure out our own journey in life. Some people have better starts than others, and some of those great starts may finish worse than individuals with a less impressive start. It all comes down to you making the best decisions for *your* life.

Some of the things that have happened in your life will be difficult to forget. There are ways to combat these thoughts and feelings when they pop up out of nowhere. When I have negative thoughts about how people wronged me, I quickly set my mind to doing bigger and better because the best revenge is success.

There are also some physical things you can do: Go running, biking, swimming— whatever is more positive than sitting around drowning yourself in sorrow. Some people try to escape reality and that's where the drug and alcohol problems present themselves. Build yourself emotionally, physically, and psychologically. If you allow someone to continue to have power over you because of a past situation, then that person or situation has won because that anger, sadness, and emotional baggage will do nothing but destroy you.

Sometimes, you can be loyal to a fault. Oftentimes, we are loyal to the wrong people and situations. Growing up in the inner city, you have all these codes and street morals that promote negativity. This mindset breeds a sense of loyalty that is pure but wrong because you are traveling down a road that is filled with negativity and everyone who condones this behavior is just helping to sink the ship you are all on. If the goal is to have a better quality of life, some of those past experiences and people will have to be left where they are—especially if you cannot convince them to change their negative ways.

Try to reach back to help others who may not see the light, but never be loyal to a disloyal cause. Don't get caught up in this. It promotes standing up for someone when they are wrong. It promotes not calling out a person who is bringing down the community with criminal activity. It's not realistic to think the past won't visit you from time to time, but don't live in it. Compartmentalize the people, places, and things that take you down a dark path, and leave them there as a reference in case you need to be reminded of the life you do not want.

Do not give negativity any permanent place in your life. You will learn to recognize negativity throughout your life, but learn where it comes from sooner than later. Some people are not good for your growth, and you have to let them go their own way. There are places inside and out of your neighborhood which are not conducive to success. There are certain things you may want to be a part of that promote negativity. Let them go. This is where mental and emotional toughness comes into play. There is always a choice to be positive, which is a way out of the cycle. The way out is through *you*! We have to rage against the machine that continues to claim lives and stunt growth. Don't let the world eat you up before there is an opportunity for you to learn who you truly are and the amazing impact you can have in this world.

Growing up poor and not having enough money to purchase the latest designer clothes was tough, but what was worse was struggling with utilities and keeping food on the table. This was disheartening, even though my parents did the best they could...most of the time. There were plenty of times we didn't have to go without lights, gas, water, or food. Most of those situations came about because of my father's mismanagement of funds due to his drug addiction.

Since good jobs were scarce, many people in my community looked to selling drugs as an opportunity to not only put food on the table, but to enrich themselves and to be "somebody." Certainly, in their minds, they probably thought dealing drugs was the sole opportunity to be someone in life. The dealers were like celebrities in my neighborhood because they had lots of money, fast cars, and hot women. At the time, the drug lifestyle was very glamorous, and this made the average "working man" look foolish. What it took a working man to make in a two-week paycheck, some corner-boy teenager could make in a day.

The fast money and its lavish lifestyle hypnotized the whole country, mostly in the inner cities. Being patient for most of these people was not an option. Even with the possibility of long prison sentences, violence, and death, people were lining up to get into the drug game without thinking about the consequences of how it would destroy their families and the larger community. Most of these people had a choice to be content with less flashy clothes or cars, to work their way up, educate themselves, build a legitimate business, but they wanted instant wealth and immediate gratification. The saying that plays consistently in my mind throughout these drug-fueled years is "Rome wasn't built in a day." I interpret this saying to mean, building an empire doesn't happen overnight.

There is a huge amount of hard work and patience that goes into becoming a legitimate success. There are also certain growing pains you must endure before you achieve success. Success is what you make it, so be sure to define your success by coming up with a list of goals you set out to achieve. Once you achieve these goals, you can start building some momentum for success in all aspects of your life. Keep building on the small success blocks, to create a solid foundation that is strong so it cannot be compromised or easily destroyed.

Never try to live in someone else's expectation of what

success is for you. What I mean by this is never let someone else define success for you. I am excluding what a parent may want for you because parents are truly the first mentors and coaches you will have in life. It's because of this that I challenge parents to be present in their children's lives indefinitely whenever possible. For all current and future parents, please don't fall into the trap of believing once a child turns eighteen your job is done because that's when they may need you the most. A child will always need the steady guidance and direction from their parents, and this always has to be conveyed through love and positivity.

I was loyal to people and situations that didn't serve my purpose for too long. As I stated before, sometimes the people you need to distance yourself from are those who grew up with you. The people who have been riding next to you for years are the ones who might be terrible influences. Now, I am not saying to disown family members and friends because they are important, but if they live in negativity, separate yourself and seek out the positive support of individuals who will help you get to the next level. Now, that's awesome!

There are some family members that you will simply need to spend less time with because they don't fit into your positive life's journey. If you have a cousin who is participating in criminal activity, that's probably not a cousin you want to spend a lot of time with if you are looking to lead a positive and successful life. I would never judge a person without taking into consideration their circumstances because I've known people personally whose options were to starve or to steal. I think most people in this country would go to great lengths to feed themselves or their children if they had to. But you must draw a line. For this, I am talking about the family members who have options but choose criminal activity because they don't want to work hard and be patient.

Instead of choosing criminal activity that will end in pain and sorrow for your family, elevate in a legal way. There are plenty of opportunities for you to advance legitimately. There is no reason to choose a path of destruction that historically has proven to be ineffective and counterproductive. Ask yourself, *Why would I want to go to jail for the rest of my life, away from everything that makes me human, everything that I hold dear and love?* Elevate your level of thinking. Part of this thought process is putting someone else before your own needs and desires. Before you do something that can derail your life, think about all the people who will be affected by your action, and then elevate.

Escape Through Logic & Reason

In order to flee dire and inescapable situations life presents, you must use your brain. Logic and reasoning must be a part of your thought process in all life scenarios. Developing an ability to be logical and reasonable throughout life is executed by educating yourself. If you can't read or write, you will not be able to perform either. One of the reasons so many young people—especially minorities—are killing one another and going to jail at such a rapid rate is because they lack the skills of logic and reason.

Logically speaking, a person should know that "If I kill someone for any reason other than self-defense, I am most likely going to prison for the rest of my life." On the other side, using reasoning, it doesn't make sense to shoot a person over a dirty look or a pair of gym shoes. Too many young men and women are going into prison too young for the rest of their lives because they lack these soft skills. Logically, if you go to school and get an education, graduate from high school, go for a trade or on to a university to obtain a degree, that individual should have a good chance at a decent life. No lengthy prison sentences, bullet wounds, or other violent traumas should be in your future.

If you can't stay away from bad energy because of negative people or a person in your household and neighborhood, it may be more difficult but look for any positivity that you can align yourself with in order to escape. There is a moral compass that is a part of our being that notifies the spirit when something is not right. If you follow that compass, the opportunity to make the right decision increases tremendously.

I will admit, there was always something inside of me that wanted more. There was an inner voice that was telling me I was special. Find that voice within yourself. To the parents reading this book, remember it starts with the initial love of parents. You can instill educational values during your children's formidable years of elementary school which can shape and mold their love for learning. Think of this as laying the initial bricks for a paved road to success. In order for the kids in your community to be around positive people 24/7, parents have to be that first example of what positivity looks like. The first line of defense to pour love and positivity into a child's life starts at home. Once I became a father, my dad would tell me, "Mother and father means GOD on the tongue of all children." In the beginning, a parent is "GOD" to a child before they can even fathom or develop a concept of GOD being a higher power.

Think about it: A small child relies on the parent for everything to survive so that mother or father is a focal point for growth. If a child is raised by a negative person who sits around and views the world from a pessimistic perspective that energy will eventually stain the spirit of that child. This message is for all parents and those who will become parents eventually: Whether you are old or young, your children need you to pour positivity and love into them. You can grow a weed or a beautiful flower, the decision is yours. Flowers are beautiful and most people enjoy them, but weeds are ugly and everyone is trying to get rid of them. Weeds choke the life out of everything beautiful that is attempting to grow around them. Raise flowers, not weeds, so that your community can grow healthy and strong. Success is setting a goal and achieving it. I will forever be grateful to my parents for the initial push to make education a priority in my life. I encourage all parents to make education a priority. Instead of doing something fun and frivolous or nothing at all, take your children to the library for a couple hours one weekend. Students, if you are old enough, make sure you go sit at the local library and read. Learn something new every day. Read constantly. Never stop. Don't be an average student. Go after greatness!

Some students have a greater capacity for learning. Maybe they have a photographic memory which helps them on exams, and that's great. But, if you don't have that capacity, it just means you have to work harder. Work hard to be the best student you can be and I guarantee things will start to happen for you. Teachers will notice, and family will be proud of your journey. Being intelligent is awesome! Never let anyone else make you feel inadequate because you are smart. Smart is cool; being uneducated is whack!

When I was growing up, you had to conceal your intelligence because nobody liked a "Know It All." Being studious was frowned upon by most kids—especially bullies. The probability of getting bullied was higher if you were studious. Unfortunately, these same issues still remain today. This is a backwards way of thinking because we need smart people to innovate and move the world forward. If you are growing up in an environment that makes you feel inadequate for being smart, fight for your gift because once you become an adult, being intelligent is your key to prosperity and that's gangsta.

Even if you have to execute covertly to avoid situations, you must be smart. It's not easy being the smart person in your neighborhood because others will simply not like it. It is terrible that a young kid or adult cannot shine completely in some environments. There will be people in your path who do not want you to be great. Somewhere in their process they were failed by someone, something, or even themselves. Do not make the same mistake if you have the opportunity. The people who want you to join them in misery need to be left alone especially if there is no hope to convert them to positivity.

Embrace your talents because it creates value in the world. Once you create value for yourself through education or a unique skill, there will be a demand for you in the marketplace creating an opportunity to elevate financially. Your education, skills, and experience can even assist you with starting your own business or becoming an entrepreneur. An education will help you live better than the street guy who has the money, designer clothes, cars, and rims. An education will help you obtain all those things minus the stress of police and individuals who want to rob you or worse. Street guys have to constantly look over their shoulders, and although it appears they have it all, it's just an illusion. Lives are forever changed in the streets because people want riches instantly. In life, there is no shortcut to prosperity.

The majority of people have to get up every morning

and work toward a goal. To think that you can live like P-Diddy without putting in the work like he has over the years is absurd. Put the work in and you will have your own paradise. Remember, success is a state of mind so your goals may be different from Diddy's but if you reach a goal that you set, then you are a success. Start with a short-term goal of educating yourself. Go to school, because that's the key to freedom. Education exposed me to a new world, provided freedom from a bad situation, and ultimately it saved me. Education offered a journey toward a better quality of life with meaningful relationships and experiences. I met my wife at a college function, so higher learning has been a blessing, and it will work for you as well.

One of the biggest pitfalls to avoid while living in any community is being inserted into the criminal justice system. Every day poor decisions are made which land too many individuals in the prison system. At all times, you must avoid negative contact with the police by approaching life with positivity and good choices. If you are faced with a decision that will heighten the probability of police contact in a negative way, deploy an exit strategy. Exit out of that scenario right away because your freedom and life are too valuable. You must see the value in yourself and recognize situations and scenarios that can be detrimental to your life at all times. What people think of you doesn't matter in every situation, but in order for the world to see value in your life, you must first exude importance of self. Self-love plays a major part in making decisions involving people and situations. Love yourself enough to turn down friends or family that wants to place you in harm's way.

There are an infinite number of examples throughout the world where people unnecessarily got involved in crime and situations that either ruined them or placed their lives on hold for a long time. Recently, I was scrolling through a social media site and realized that a judge had sentenced a rapper named Roberts Williams (stage name Meek Mill) to a two-to-four-year prison sentence for a probation
violation. I've followed Meek's career since he first became a mainstream hip-hop success. I was glad to see a young man from Philadelphia make it out of a bleak situation to become a star. That's what intrigued me about the young artist because pulling yourself out of the devil's belly is no simple feat.

Unfortunately, Meek was unable to leave the streets unscathed because he was facing a gun and drug possession charge from a time before many people knew him as the artist he is today,. He had to serve almost a year in jail due to these charges which initially set his music career back. Eventually, he was released and signed a record deal with Rick Ross. Because of his insertion into the criminal justice system, he would be on probation from the time he was released to present day which is how he ultimately ended up getting the two-to-four-year sentence.

I don't know the circumstances behind Meek's old charges, but it allowed the system to sink their hooks into him, never allowing him to move around freely. Even with all his success, and being a role model for the kids from his hometown, it wasn't good enough to get him out of his probation for at least eight years.

Some will argue that murderers have been released from probation quicker than Meek was and I am sure it's true, but that's not the point I am trying to drive home. Do not get involved with the system because it doesn't love you. Having a record isn't cool if it means probation or prison. No matter what your peers are doing, don't do it if it lives in negativity. The system places constraints on you that will alter your life just like Meek's. I've watched interviews where Meek discussed his situation with probation, as he explained having to ask for permission to travel domestically and abroad. He couldn't move out of Philly because of his probation. This guy is a millionaire, his face plastered all over the Internet. He has hit songs, fans everywhere, but he has to ask permission to move around the world. It's possible money and fame could make his situation a little more tolerable, but he has the same frustrations and anger a person without his resources would experience. In Meek's case, he has money, an established business, and relationships that will assist him in his quest for justice. Someone trying to get to his position may not have the resources.

Avoid the criminal justice system because you don't want your dreams placed on hold or thwarted before you can get them off the ground. I am sure Meek would want everyone to learn from his mistakes and be free. Senseless crimes committed to impress a group of people who don't care about you or your well-being is just that: senseless. Don't succumb to peer pressure. That's so lame anyway. How can you allow someone to persuade you into ruining your life? Any person trying to coerce you into something that can lead to your freedom being taken away doesn't have your best interest at heart.

I know what some will say, "Well, Manson, what if your circumstances are so terrible that you have to steal just to feed yourself?" I've been there. It's an unfortunate reality for so many people living in poverty all around the world, so I understand that some circumstances can't be avoided. But, you have to fight the temptation to do something that can change the trajectory of your life. Don't make a temporary situation into something permanent. It's best to figure out a way to do things legally as not to ruin something that could be beautiful later on in life.

The problem with so many people is that they don't really think every thought through to its conclusion. I can hear my dad's voice constantly in my head, even as an adult, "Think every thought to its conclusion." For me, there were plenty of times in life where things were destitute. Whether it was a shortage of money or other resources essential to survival, I felt stuck. I had a decision to make, and more times than not, it was to do things right. Sure, I've made bad decisions as a young man. That's what makes me qualified to speak to you about *your* life. I've lived it. Luckily, none of my bad decisions landed me in prison.

All throughout life, you will be tested with situations that could lead to police contact or being arrested. It is in your best interest to lean on reasoning and logic in your decision making. Once a crime is committed, there are no apologies that will be accepted. Once the police are involved, there is no turning back. You cannot tell an officer that you didn't mean to break the law. The officer will not care what your life is like at home or any trial and tribulations that led you to this poor decision, however valid you may think your reasons are. The police officer doesn't always have the flexibility to consider these factors. They will not arrest you because they are bad people. It's not that they don't sympathize with your situation. The officer has a job to do, and that job is enforcing law. You break the law, you lose your freedom. Once arrested, you get processed into a system that will not let you go easily. A judge will decide your fate. If your life was riddled with unsurmountable constraints and roadblocks, most likely a judge and jury may not get to hear the full story and depending on the crime, it may not sway their perception of you anyway. If that's the case, the judge will be unaware of the heartache and pain you've endured over your life which led to your bad decision. In many cases, it will not even matter. You will be sentenced for your crime based on guidelines that were created by other human beings. Whether being housed in a prison, put on house arrest, or serving probation, your freedom to move about this earth freely will be compromised.

Once this happens, your opportunities in life start to be limited. There is a better life waiting for you outside the confines of your neighborhood, city, or state. But, if you are restricted from leaving your environment, it could place you back in the same situations that led you to make a bad decision in the first place. Sometimes these encounters end with loss of life. There have been too many instances in American history where police brutality has overwhelmingly targeted minorities, resulting in our deaths. Several of the police encounters have been caught on video and displayed on social media, and this is always heartbreaking.

The people who lost their lives in these encounters did not deserve to die. No one should lose their life senselessly, but our job is to limit exposure and mitigate risk associated with these negative encounters. Any negative encounters with police are not healthy for you or the community. Allow yourself to grow as a person before making adult decisions. Life can be tough and cruel. Those who are supposed to protect us sometimes fall short, but there are opportunities out there for you to give yourself a chance to live a life of prosperity.

Remember, a life of prosperity is not connected to materialism. I am talking about a life where you are free to do as you please with the life that GOD gave you.

Always remember, you can have a life that is fulfilled without falling into the materialism trap. Over the years, I've witnessed people lose their freedom or their lives over something materialistic. Is your life worth more than a pair of $200 sneakers? A pair of sunglasses that won't be in style next year?

Hopefully, your answer is a resounding "yes." But, if it isn't, then I am telling you that no pair of sneakers or anything that can be produced by another man or woman is worth your life or anyone else's. Once you start to place a greater value on yourself, you will start to see the world and your place in it differently. In turn, you will be less likely to commit a crime that will take your value away.

Elevate yourself and live your best, fullest life possible.

www.ingramcontent.com/pod-product-compliance
Lightning Source LLC
Chambersburg PA
CBHW062002040426

42447CB00010B/1873